VINTAGE CHRISTMAS

COLOURING BOOK

I0465364

SOME EXAMPLES OF WHAT'S INSIDE

GRAYSCALE VINTAGE IMAGES

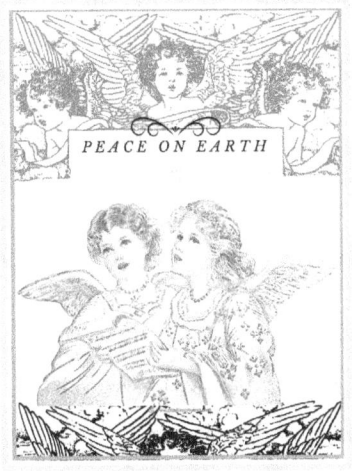
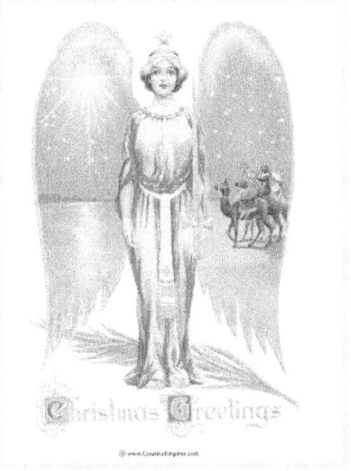
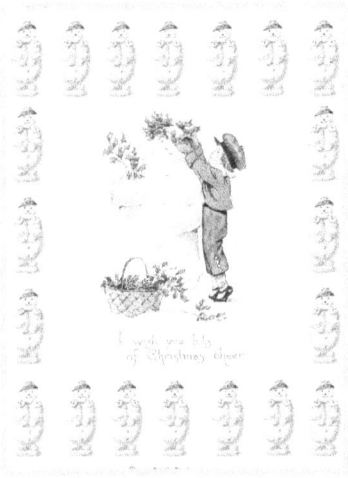

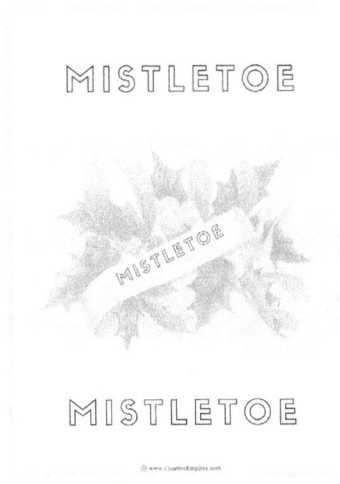
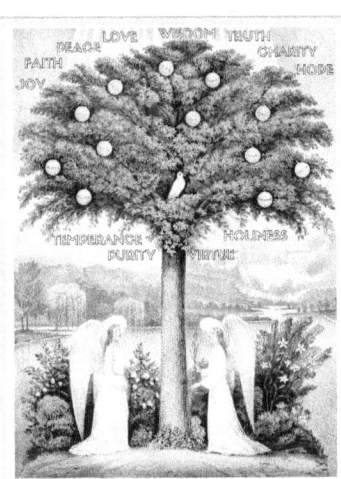
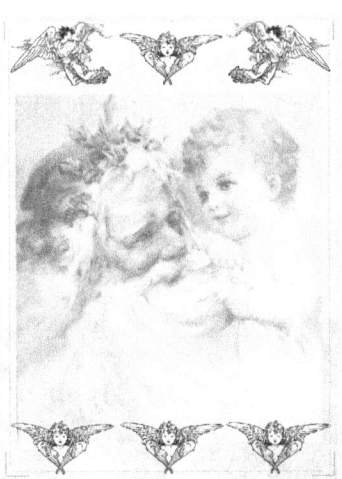

BY

CREATIVE

EMPIRES

WELCOME

To our **Vintage Christmas Colouring Book**

As a keen calligraphy hobbyist I naturally took an interest in the phenomenal growth around the world of adult colouring books. This led me to learning how to create books myself as well as also teaching and co-creating children's books with my two young sons who love this creative work too. This is their first book.

It seemed the perfect time for a revival of the art of pen to paper, with hand drawing,painting skills,colouring and more in this world of high dependency on digital gadgets.

These books are designed to enable you to immerse yourself into an often forgotten art form of using pen to paper. As well as helping with relaxation and enjoyment, drawing and colouring can help give you the well researched benefits of switching off from technology while still engaging your brain and creative mind.

Perfect Solution to Calm a Busy Mind!

INSTRUCTIONS

No instructions needed! It's your book, so you colour it,
paint it, hand doodle on it, whatever takes your creative fancy.
No rules...apart from relax!

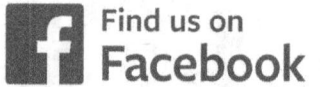 Check new books coming soon by joining our
Creative group & share your designs by uploading your pages at
www.Facebook.com/CreativeEmpires

Digital Offer
As I know we can't completely leave the digital world behind,
I'm sending the digital book copy free to Thank all customers who
have chosen this book. Shea, Rory & Tracey
ENJOY!
Please request your digital copy with the same email used for your
Amazon purchase of this book.
Email us writing DIGITAL BOOK REQUEST in the Subject line to
tracey@creativeempires.com

VINTAGE CHRISTMAS

COLOURING BOOK

VINTAGE
COLOURING
COLLECTION

All rights reserved. Creative Empires - Tracey Hurst,
Shea Hurst McGowan & Rory Hurst McGowan
have asserted their rights under the Copyright, Designs, and Patent Act 1988,
to be identified as the Authors of this work herein.

No part of this publication may be reproduced or transmitted by any means or in
any form, either electronic or mechanical, including photocopy, recording or any
information storage and retrieval systems without the prior written permission
from the Authors/Publishers.

ISBN-13: 978-1981363063
ISBN-10: 1981363068

BY

CREATIVE

EMPIRES

COLOUR TEST PAGE

www.creativeempires.com

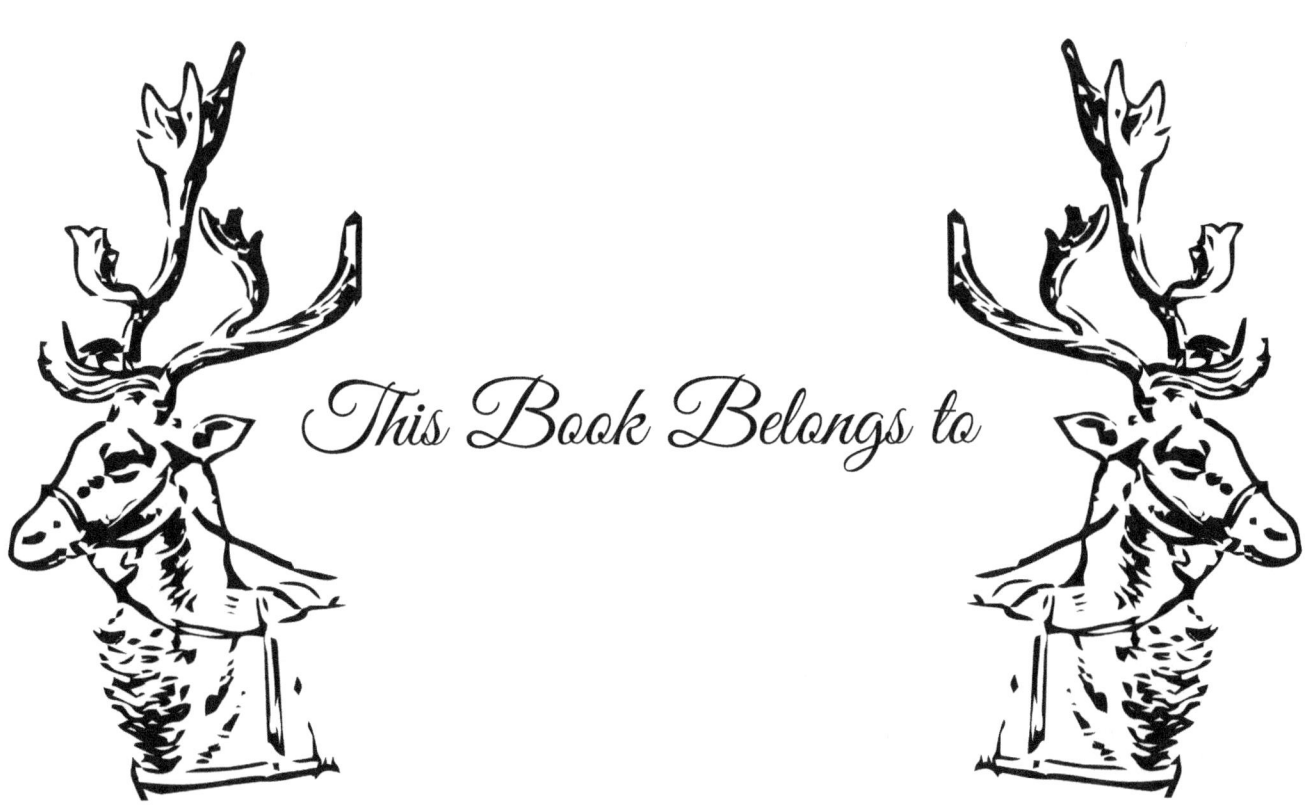

This Book Belongs to

....

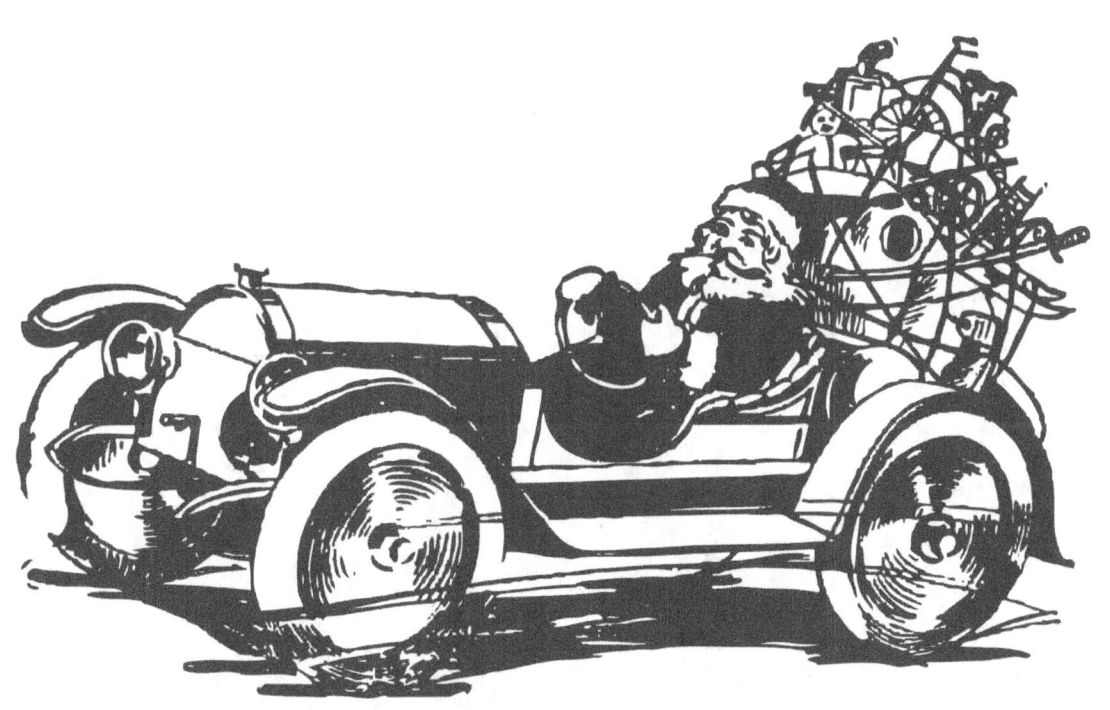

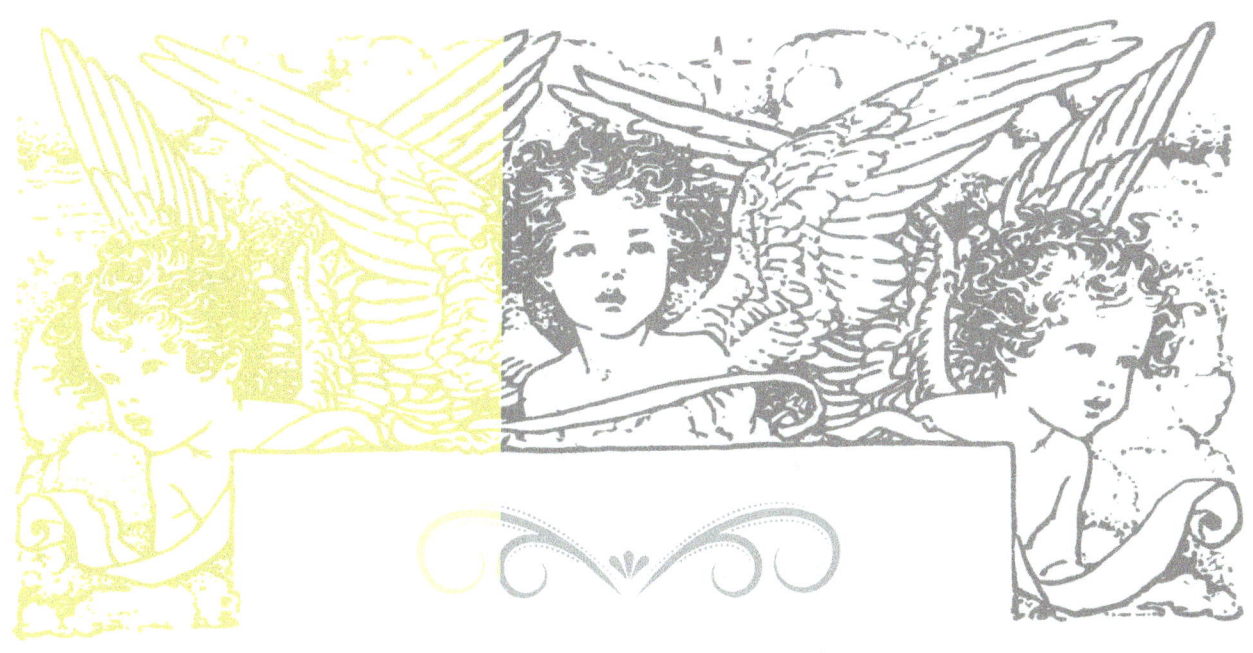

PEACE ON EARTH

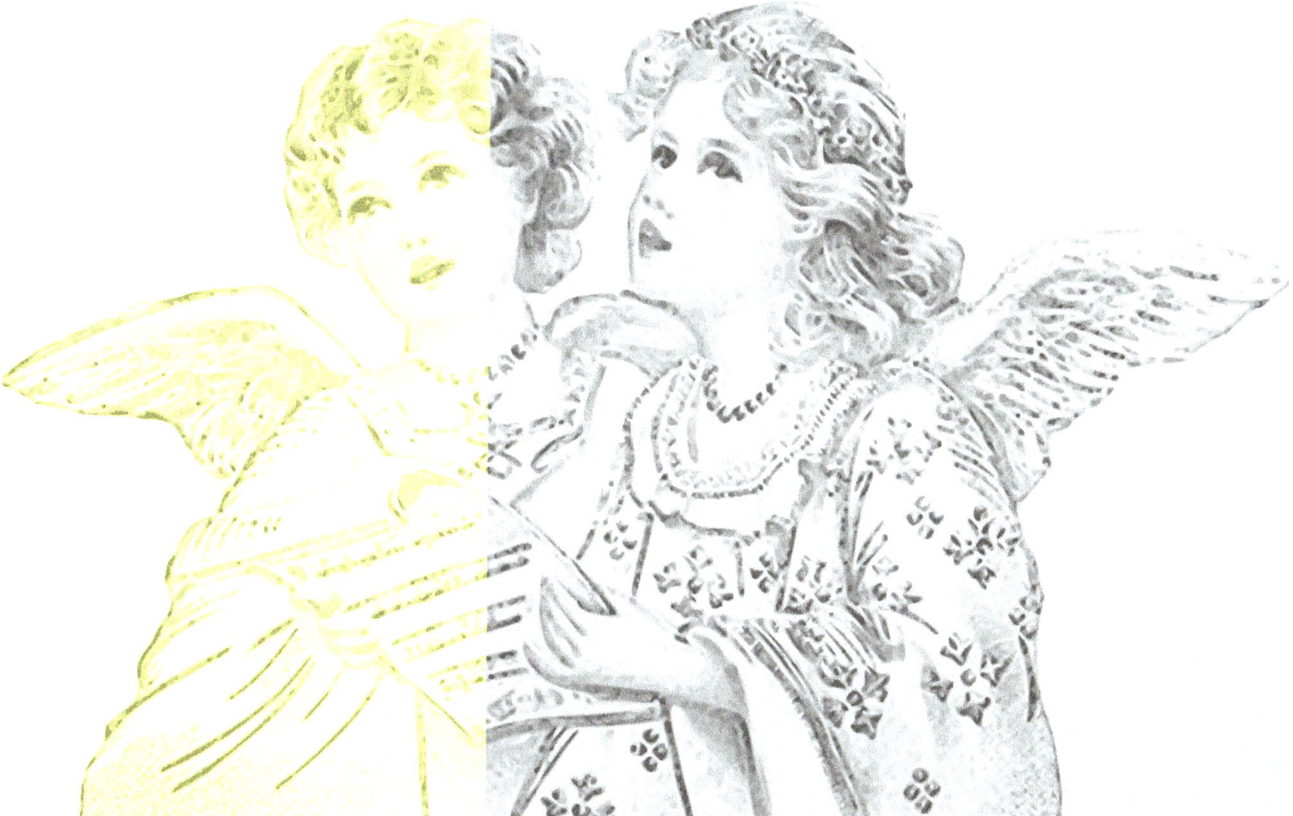

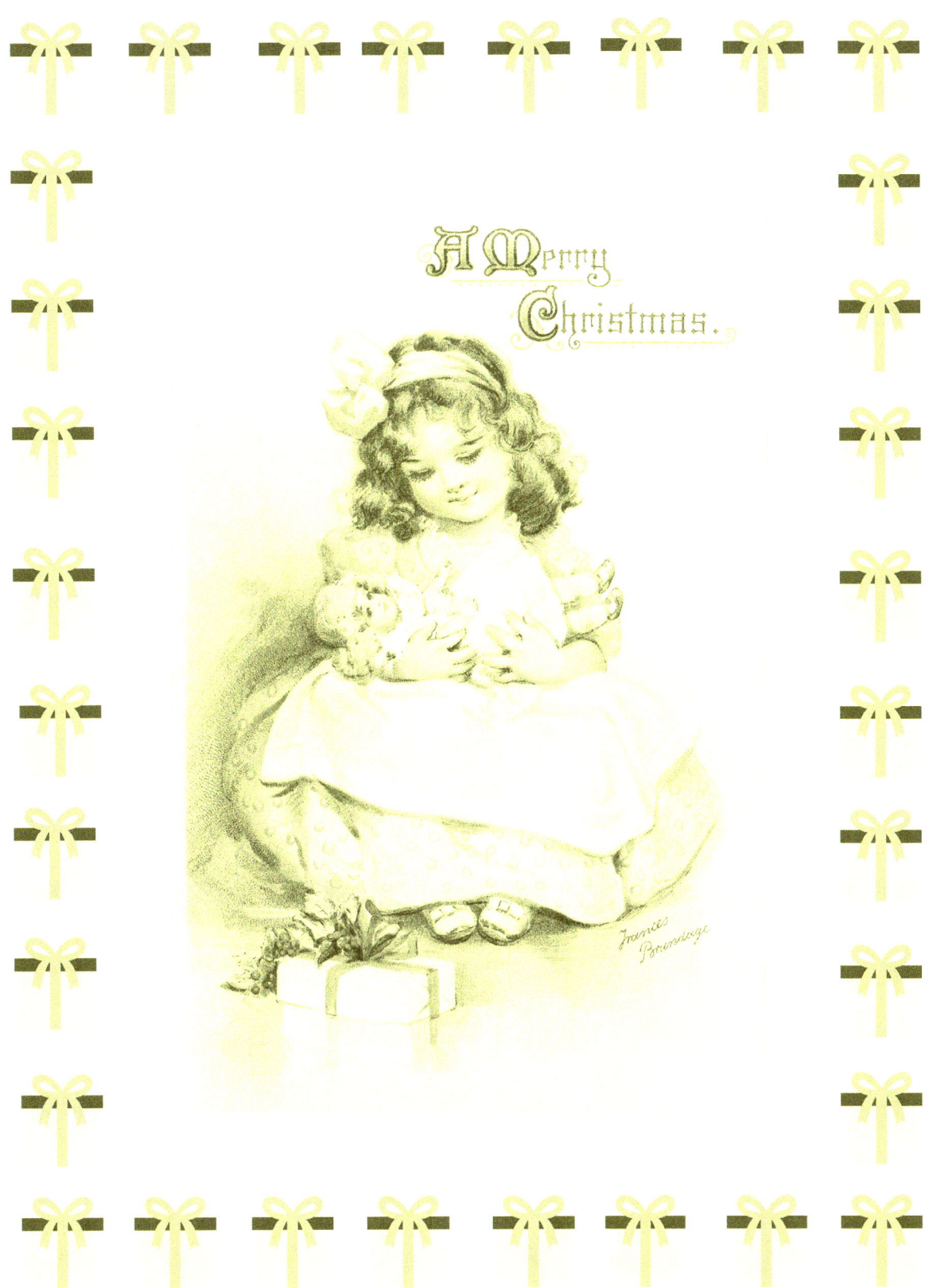

A Merry Christmas.

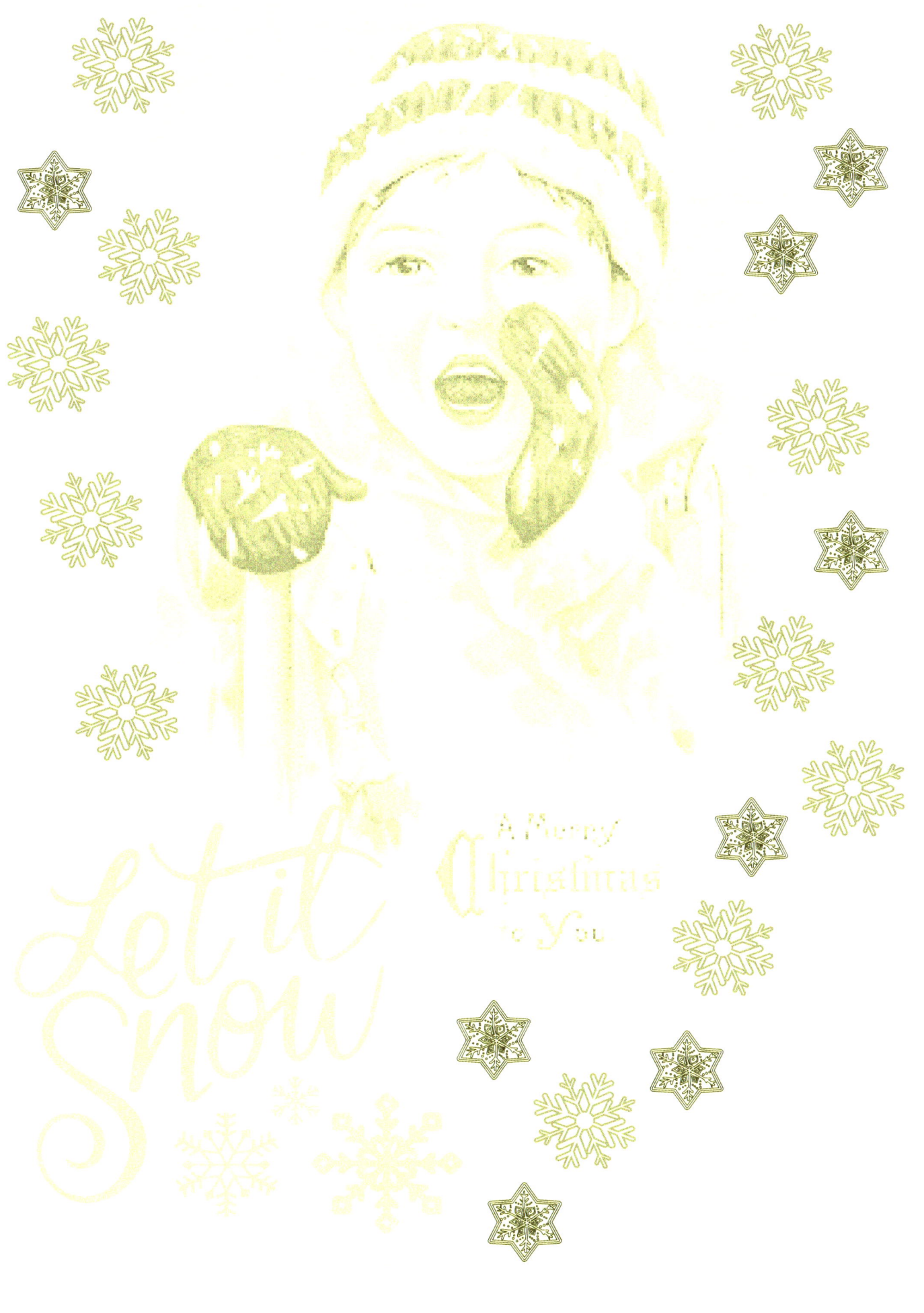

Let it Snow

A Merry Christmas to You

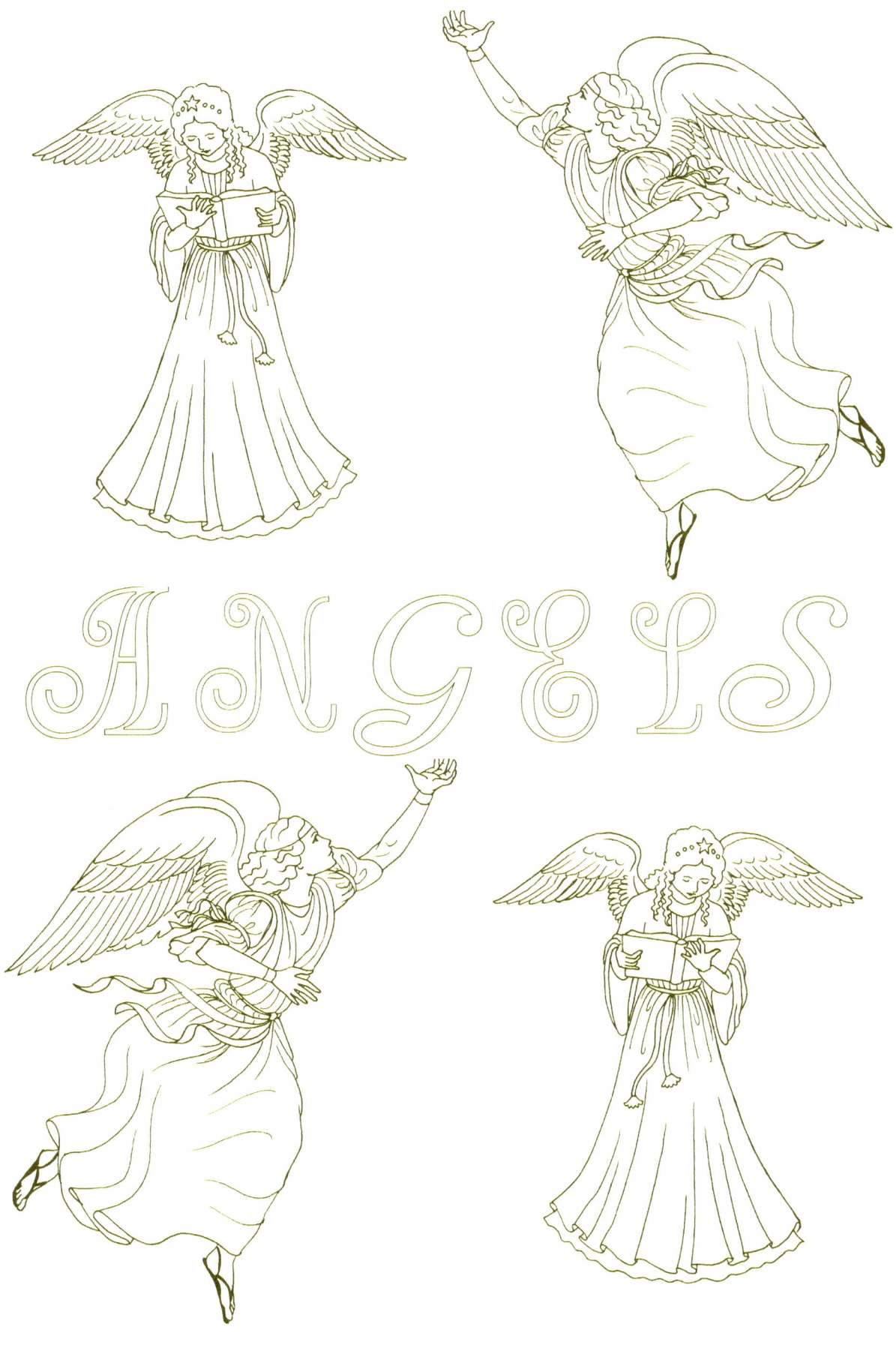

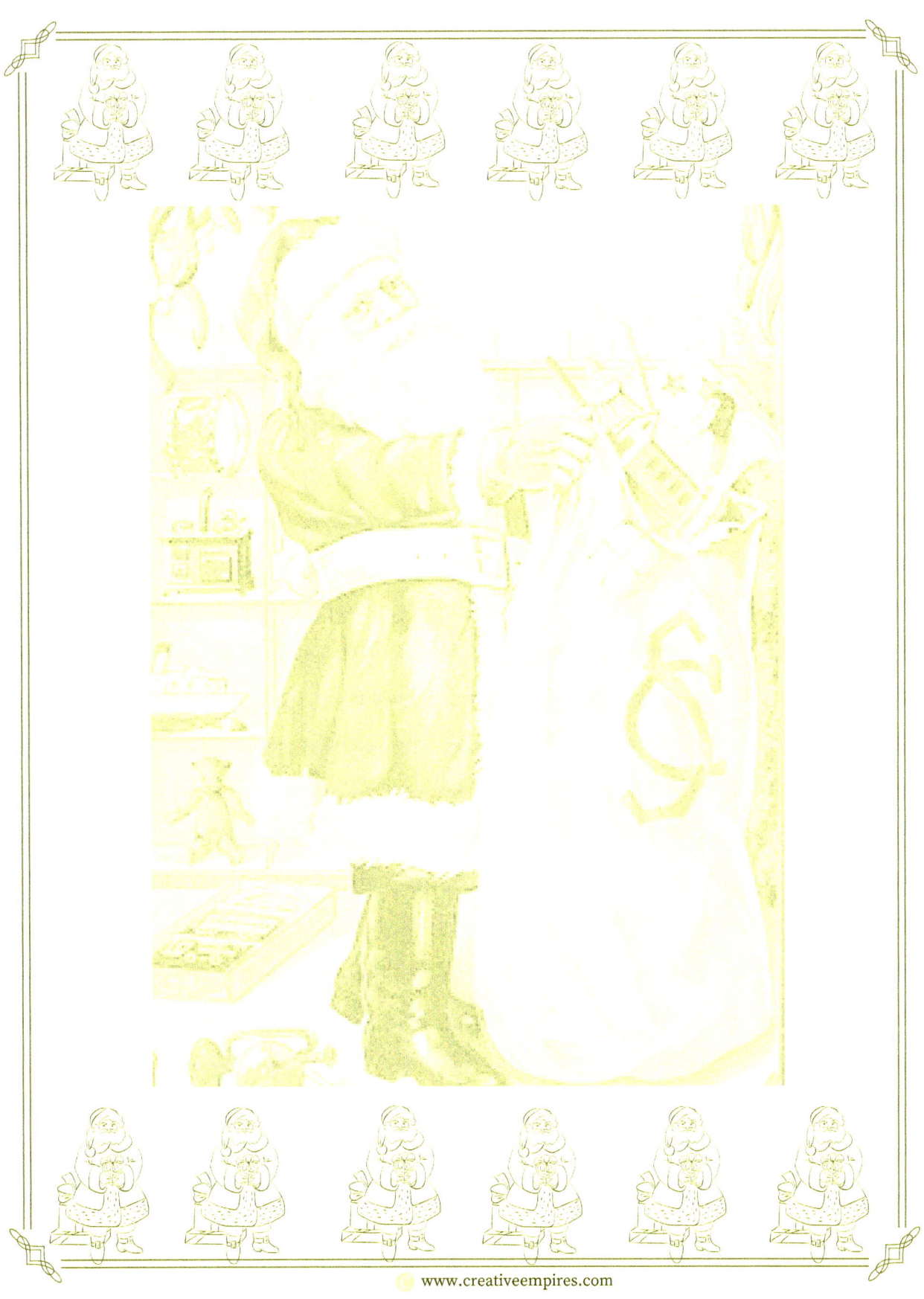

www.creativeempires.com

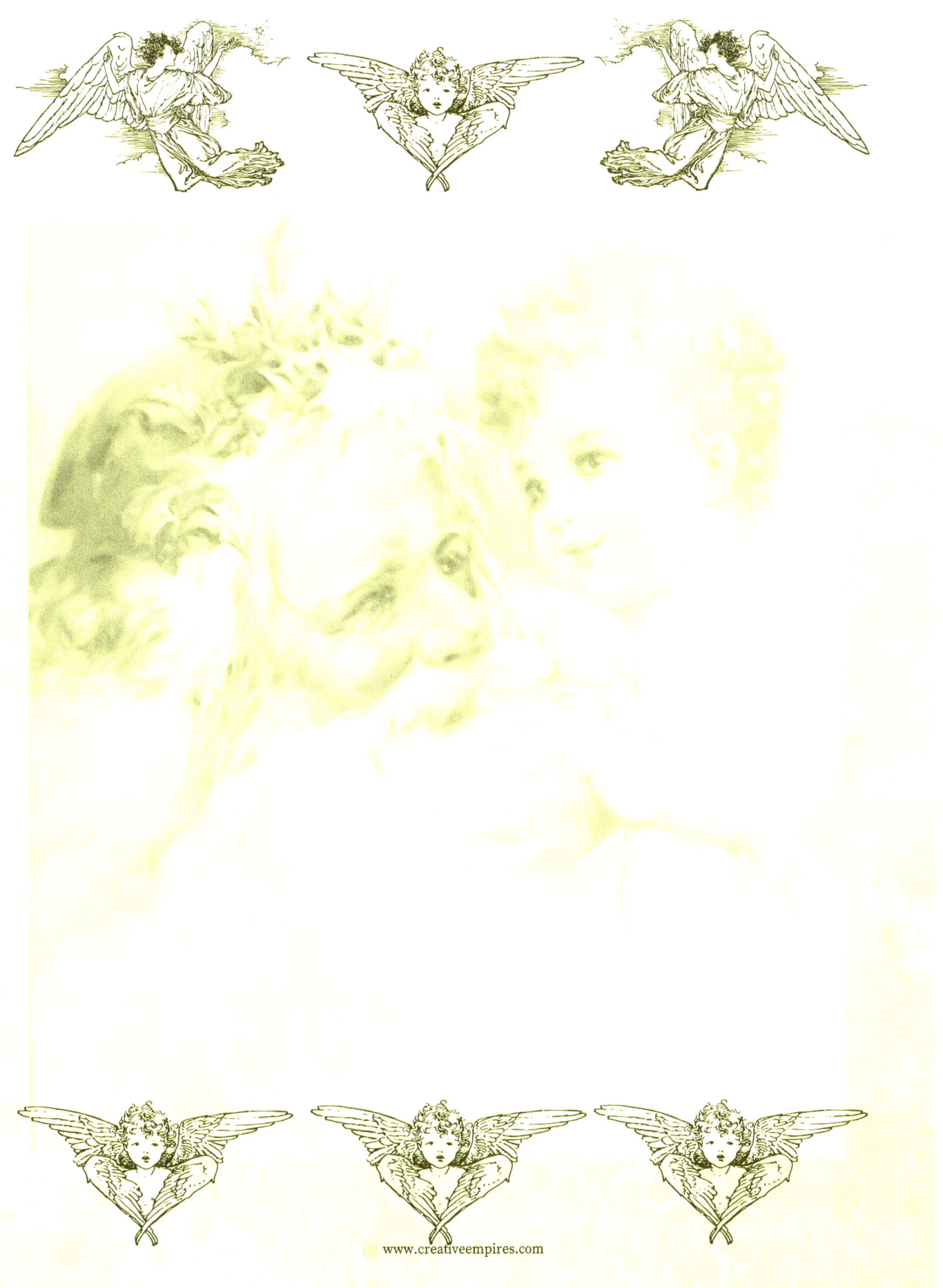

www.creativeempires.com

www.creativeempires.com

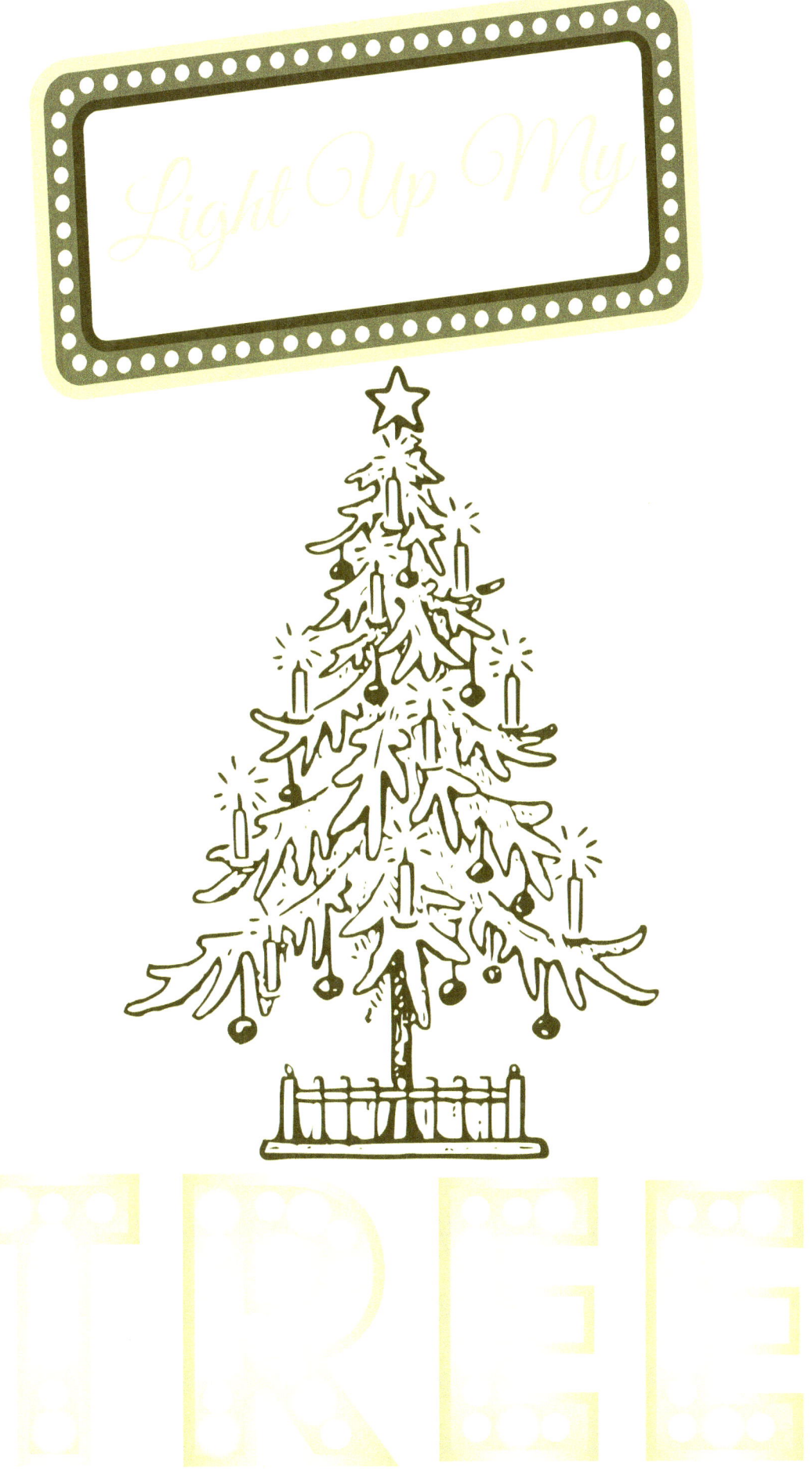

Light Up My

TREE

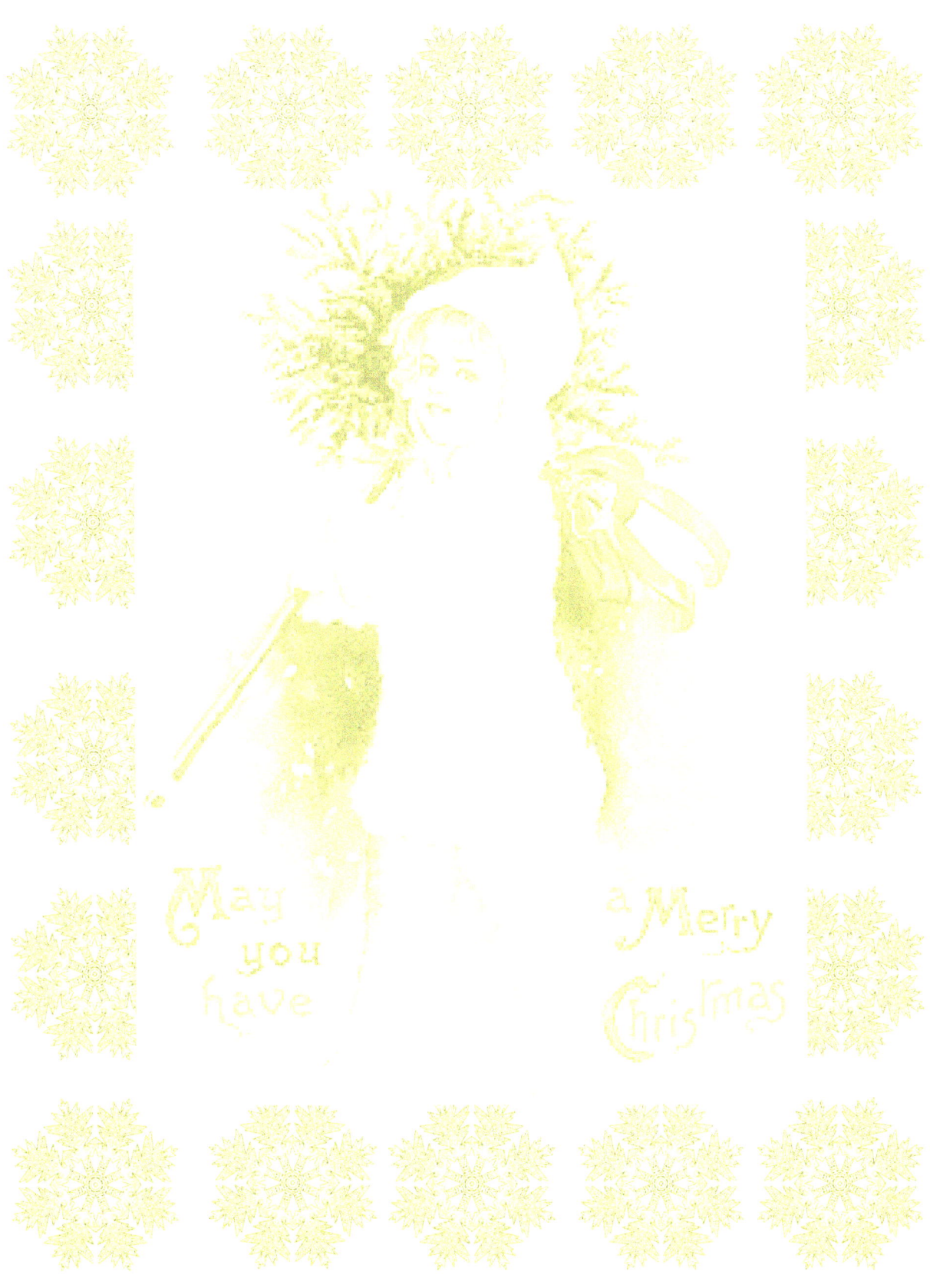

May you have

a Merry Christmas

LOVE

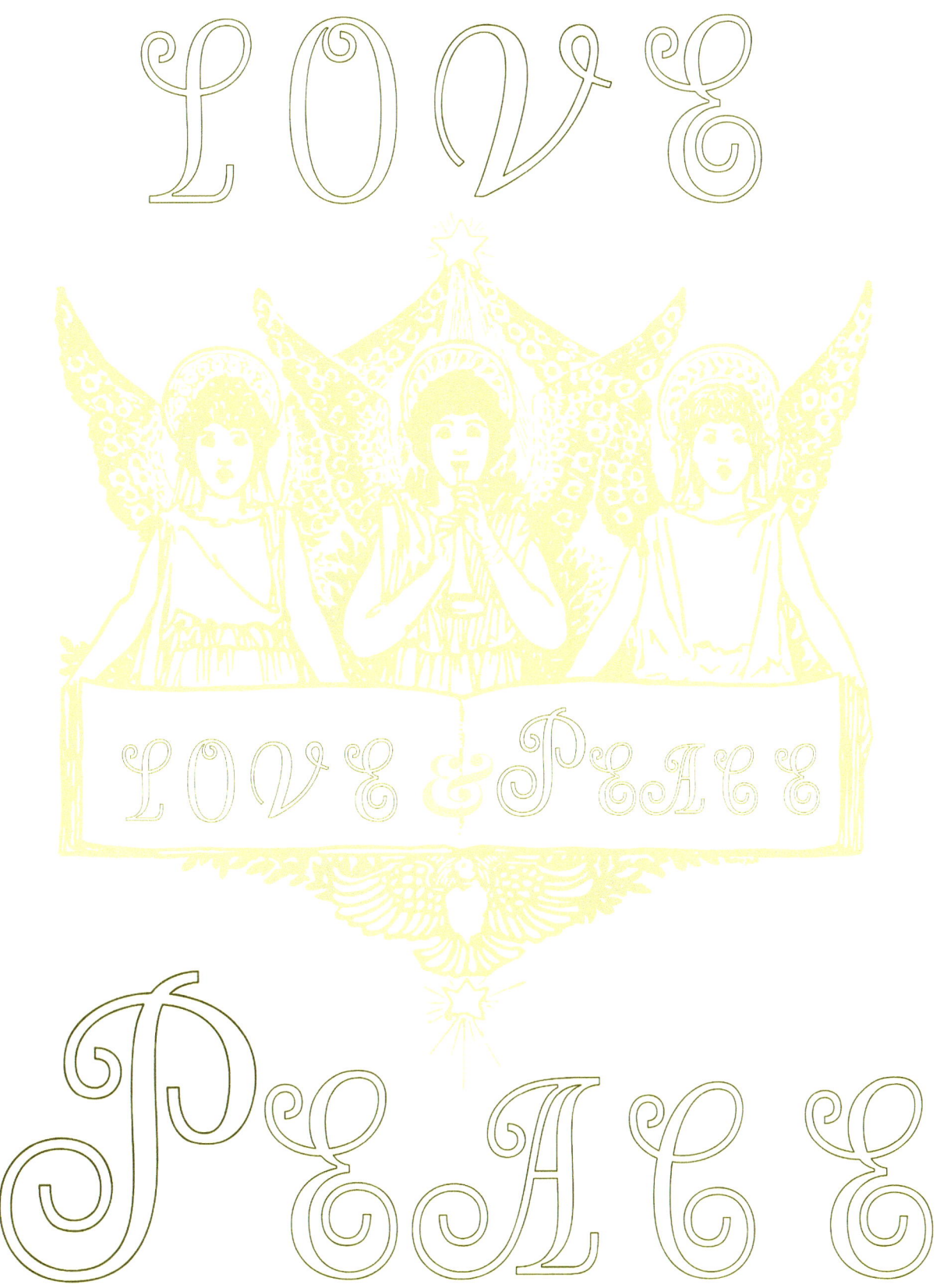

LOVE & PEACE

PEACE

HAPPY
CHRISTMAS
AND
TO ALL A GOOD NIGHT

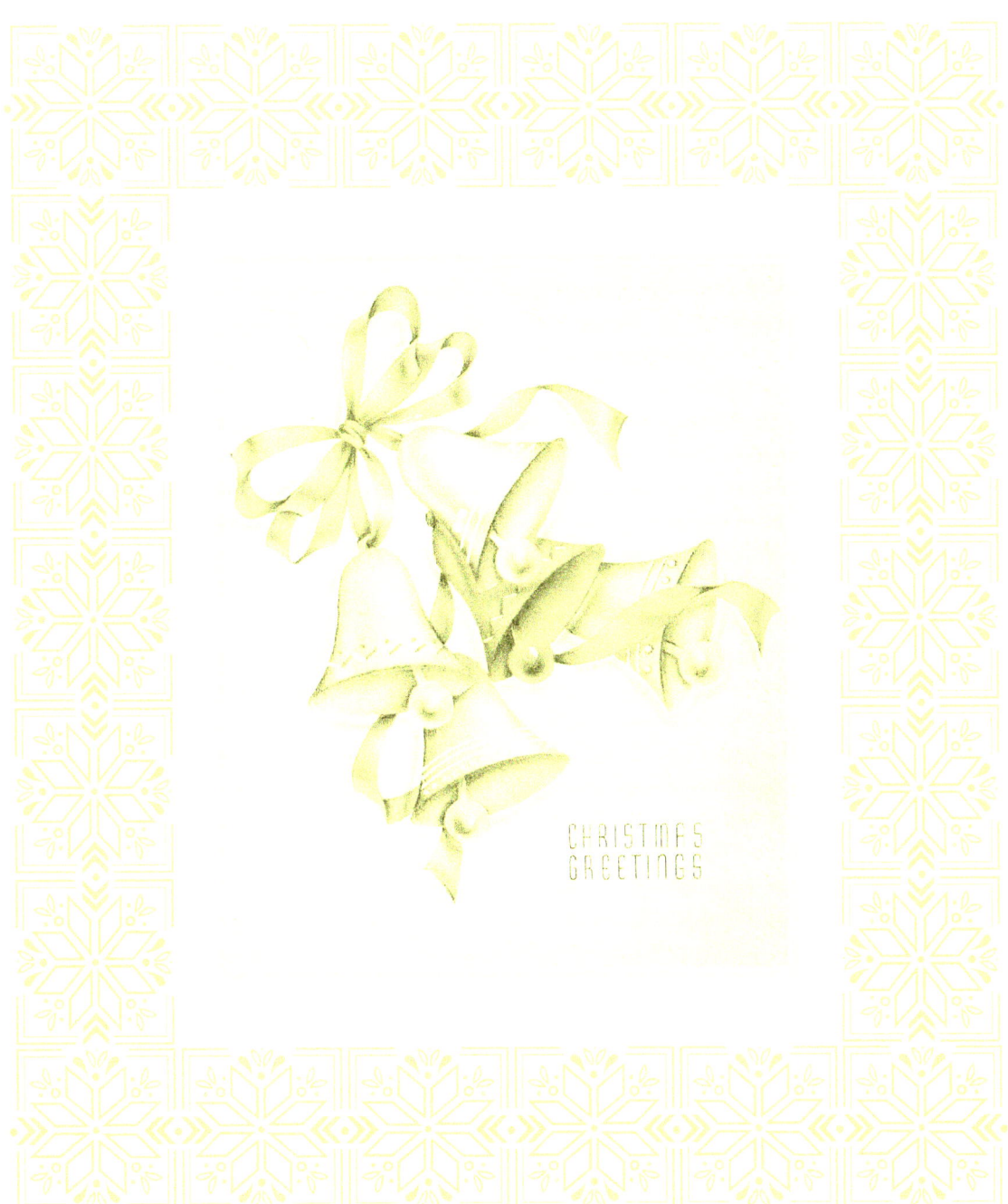

CHRISTMAS
GREETINGS

www.CreativeEmpires.com

www.CreativeEmpires.com

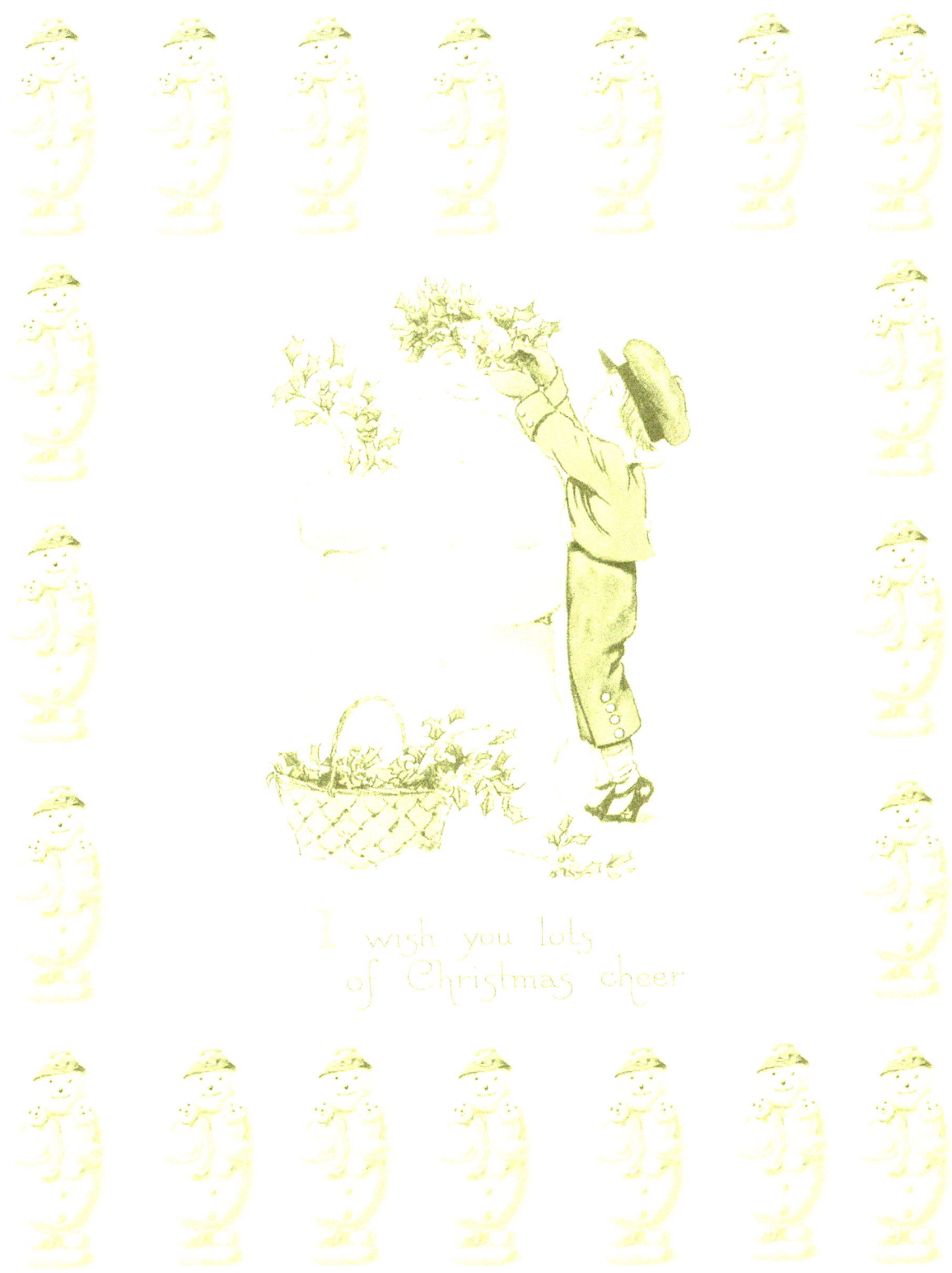

I wish you lots
of Christmas cheer

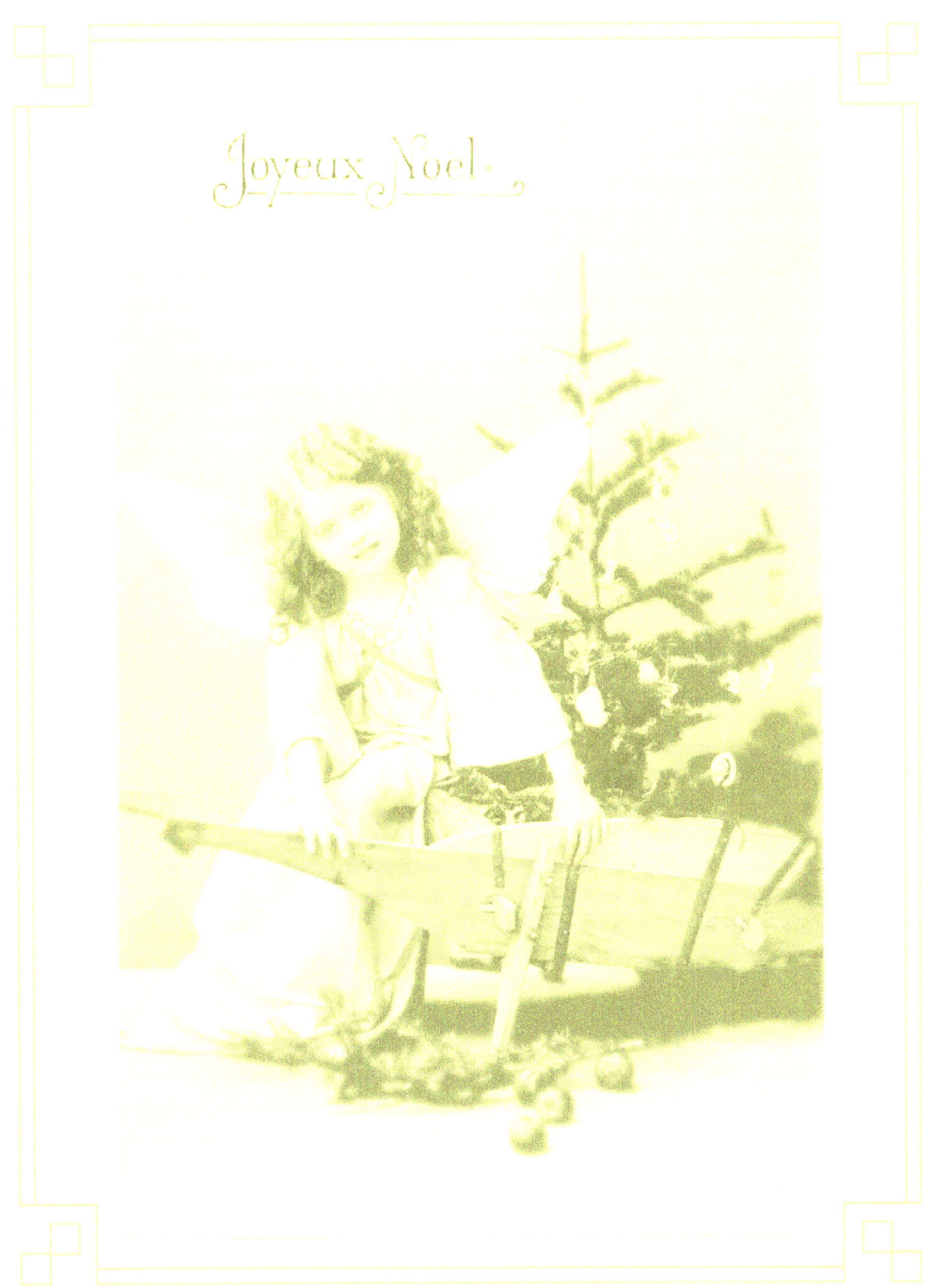

Joyeux Noel

www.CreativeEmpires.com

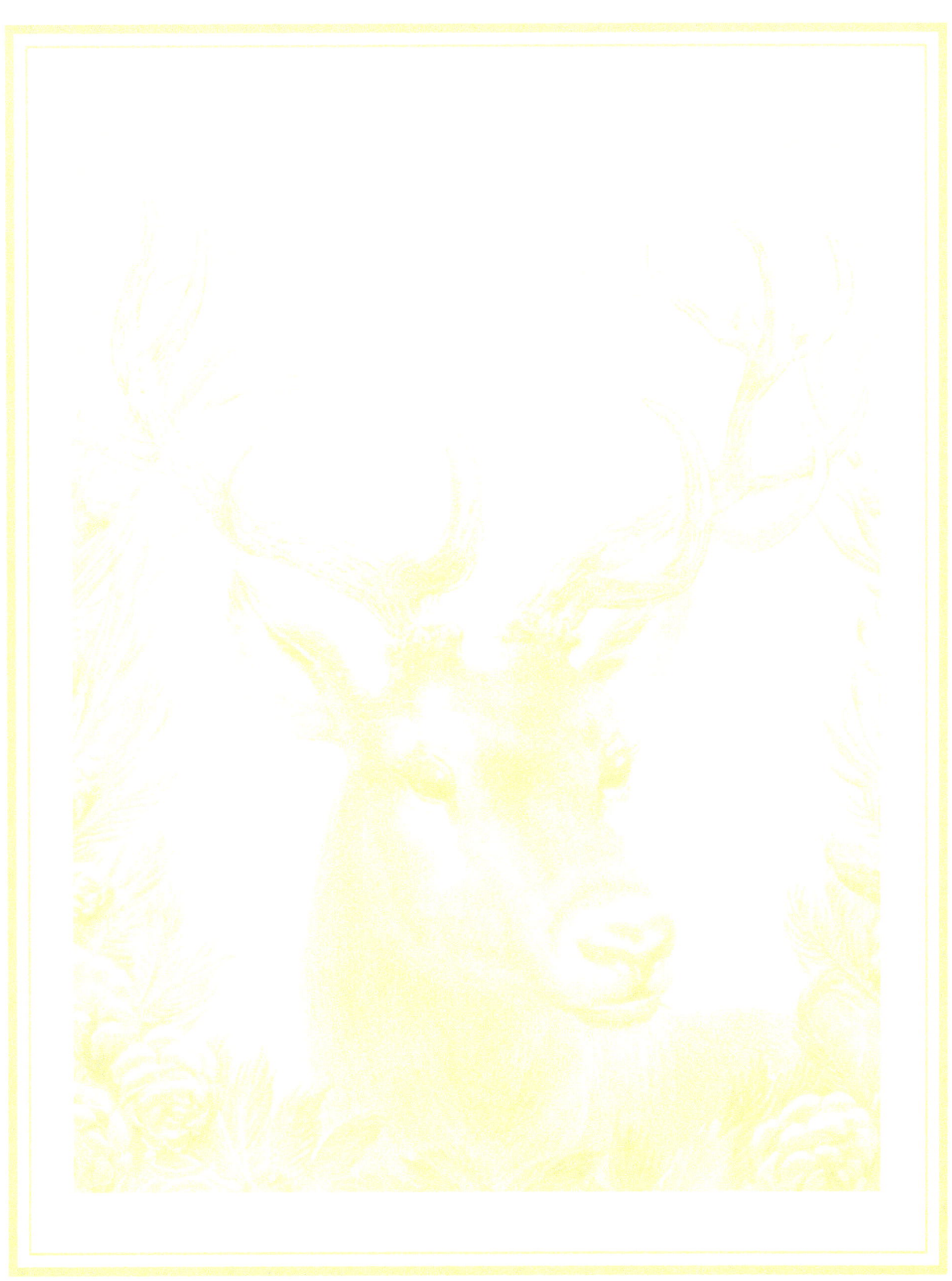

www.CreativeEmpires.com

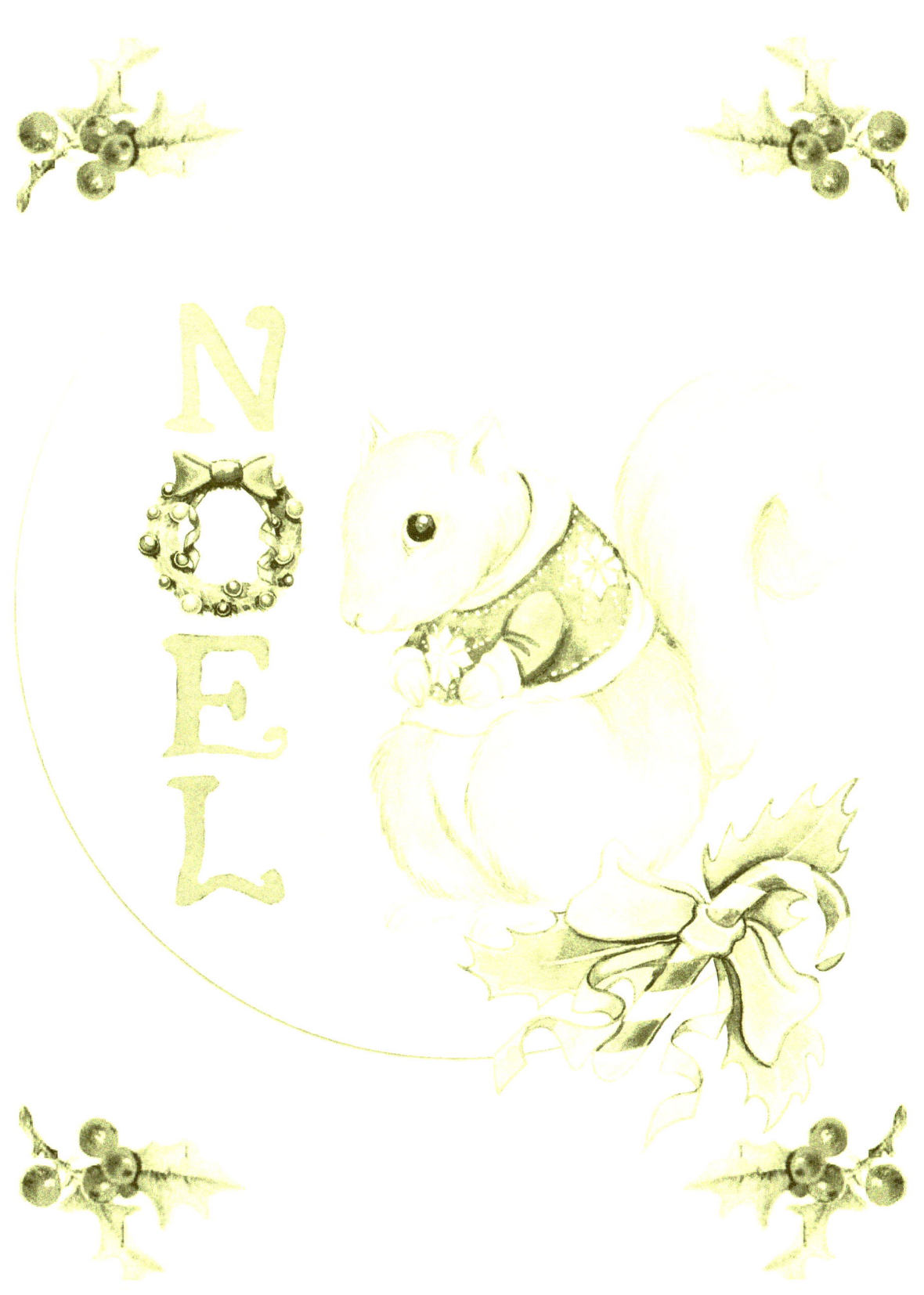

www.CreativeEmpires.com

www.CreativeEmpires.com

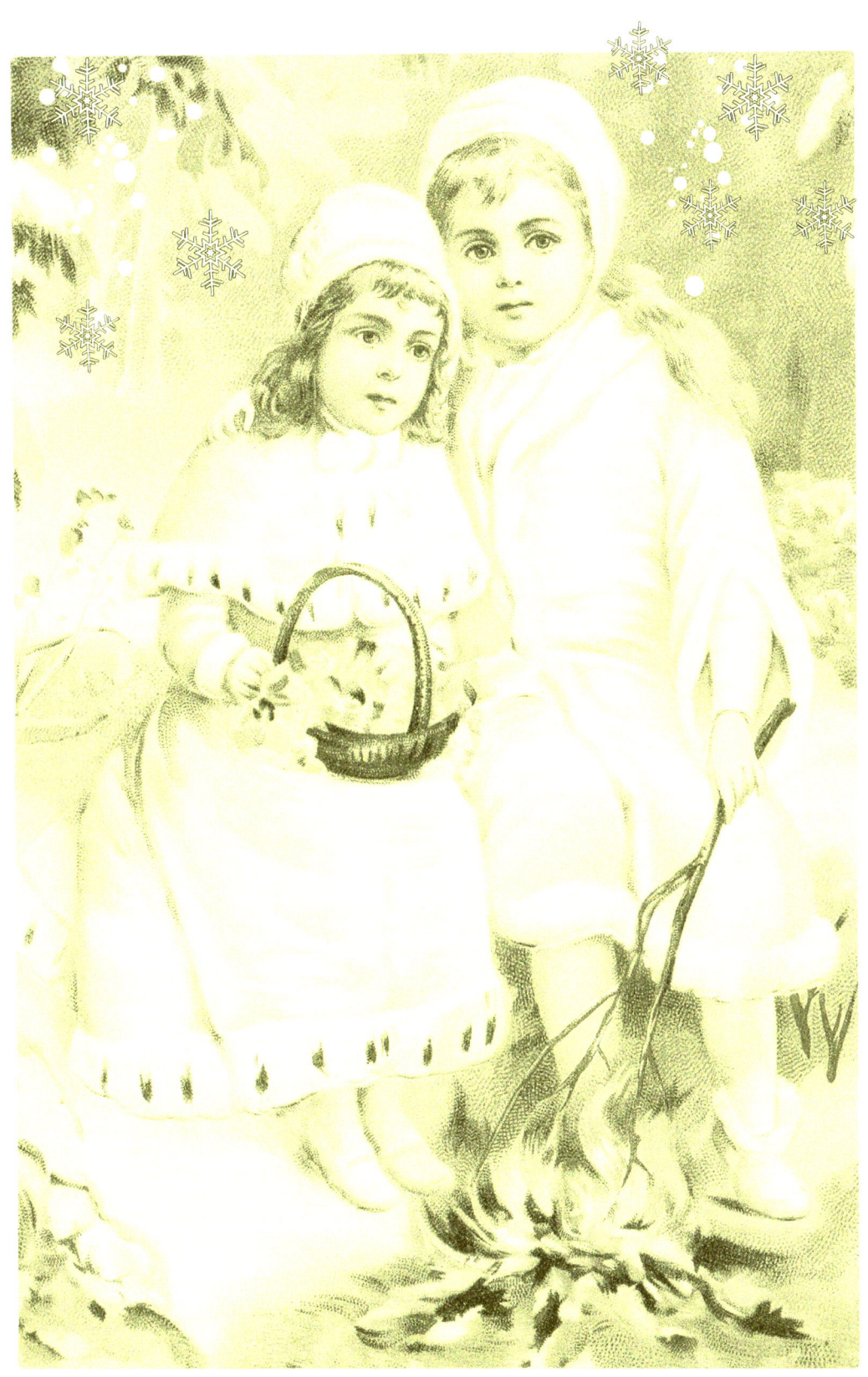

www.CreativeEmpires.com

www.CreativeEmpires.com

MISTLETOE

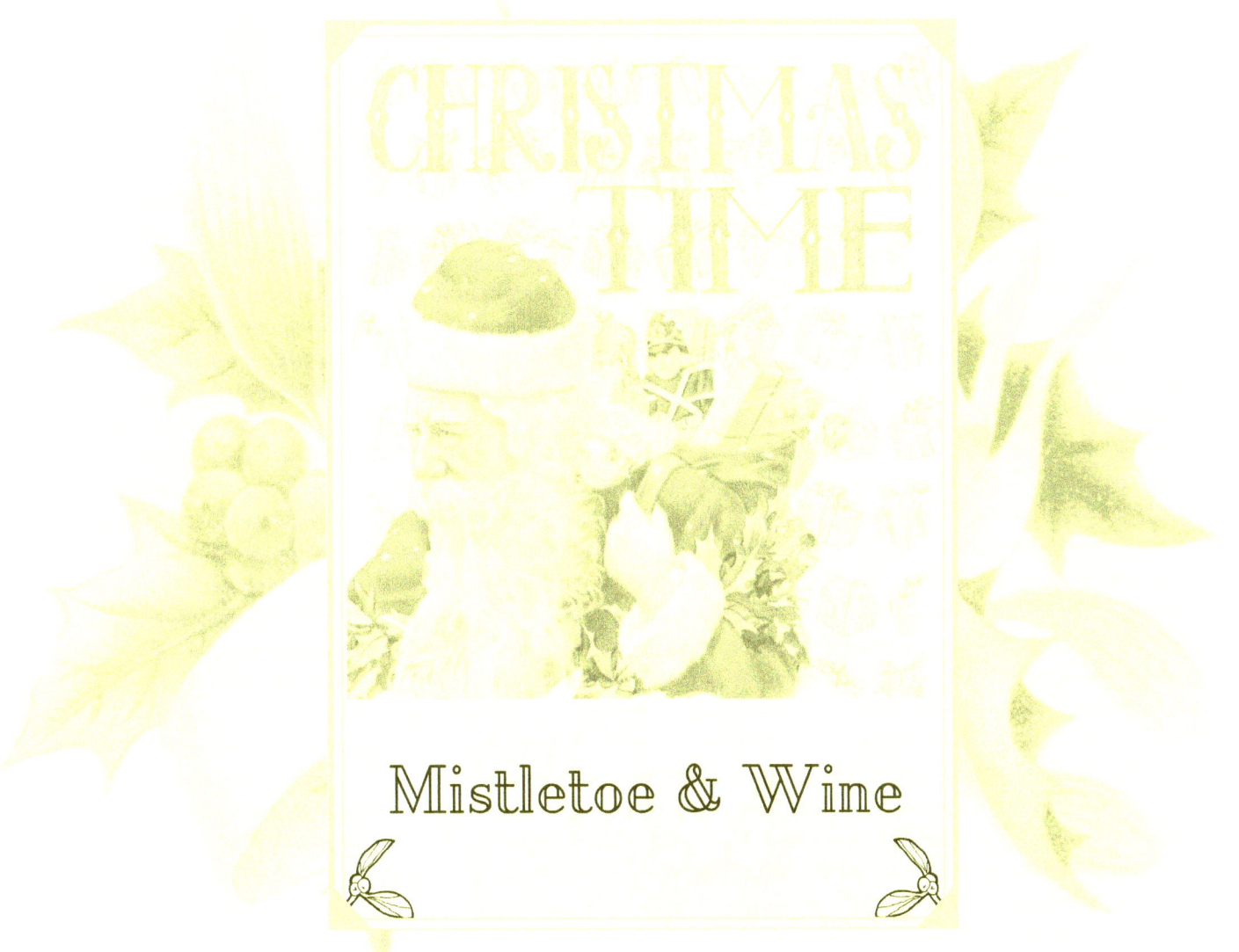

CHRISTMAS TIME

Mistletoe & Wine

MISTLETOE

www.CreativeEmpires.com

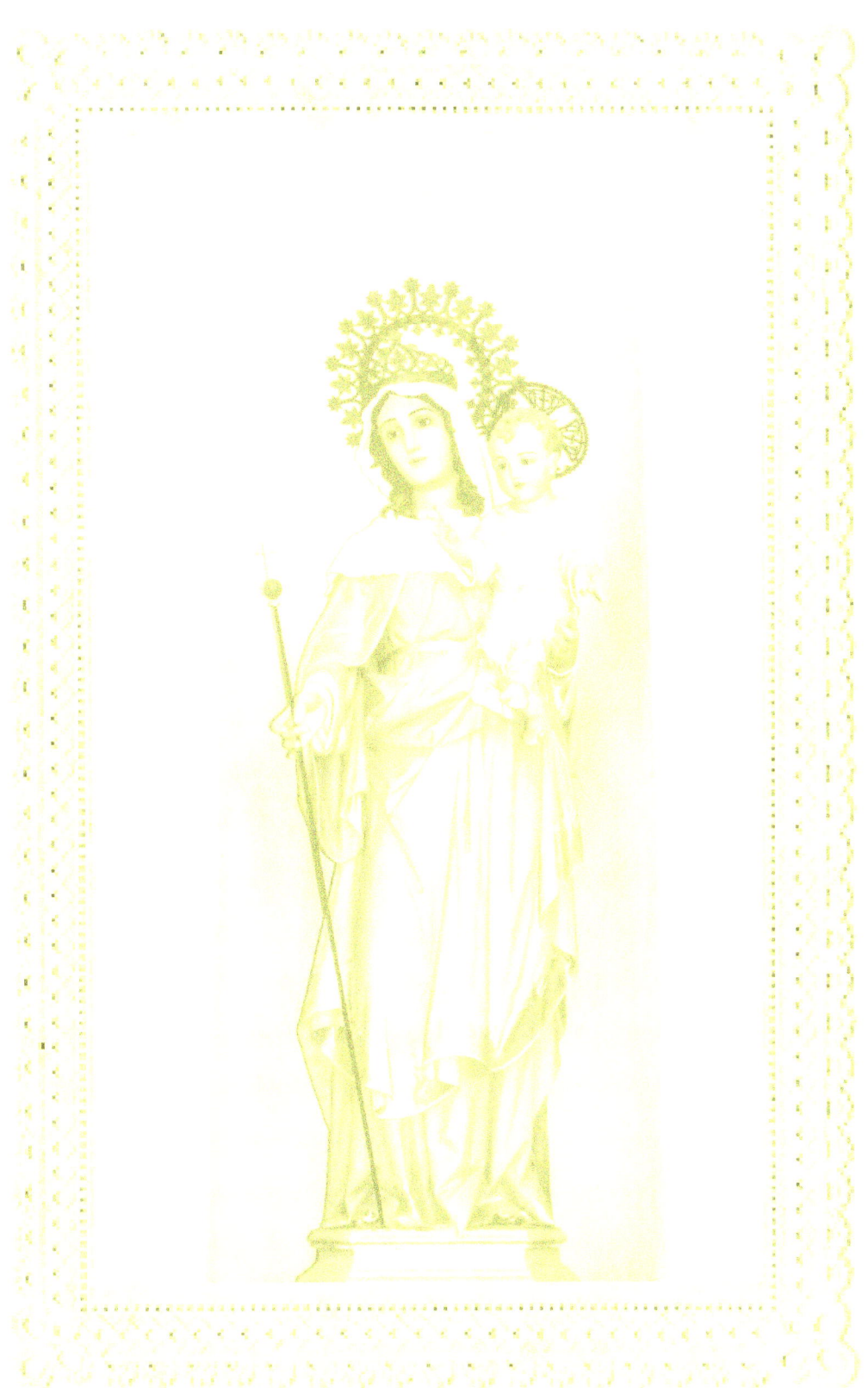

www.CreativeEmpires.com

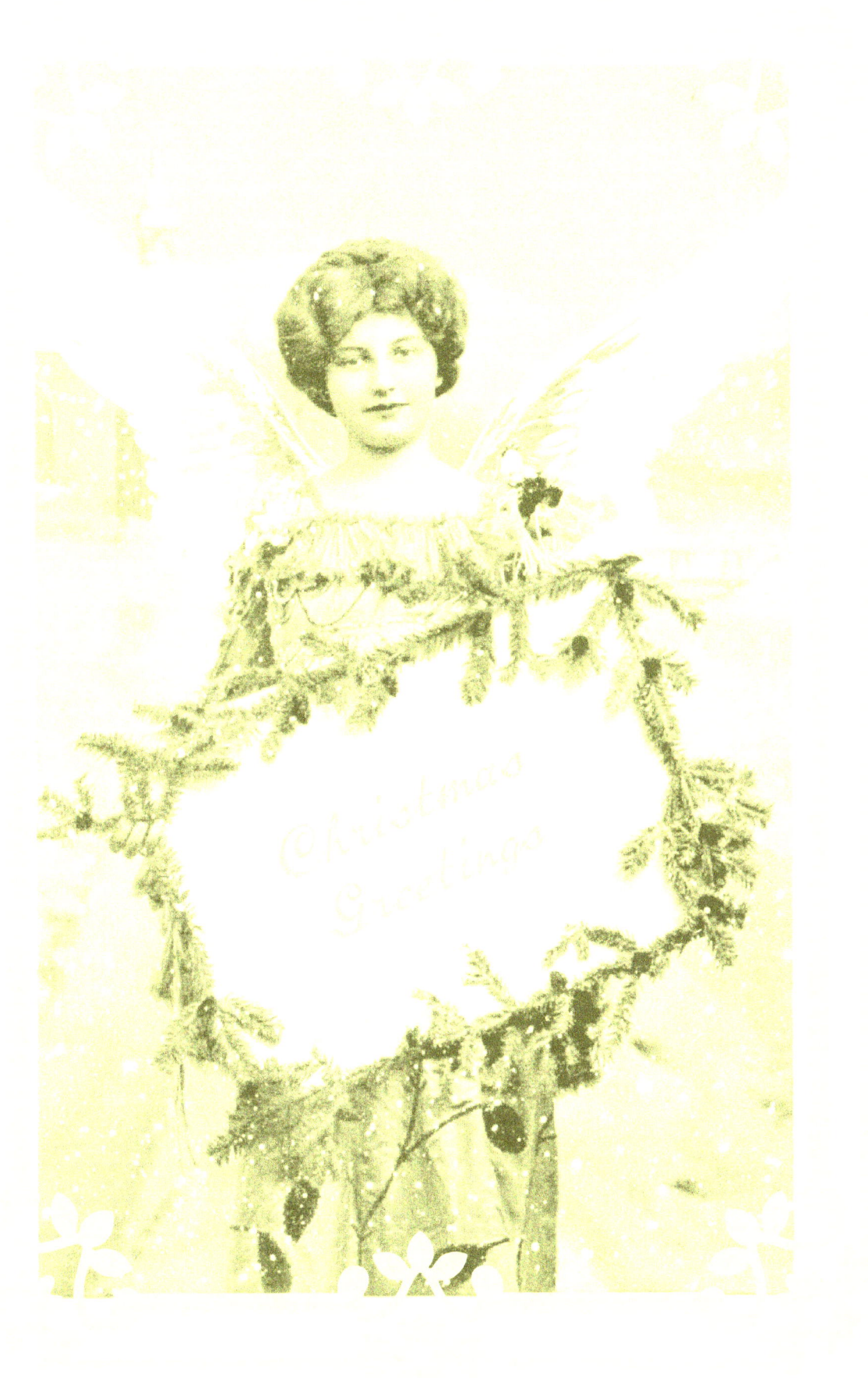

www.CreativeEmpires.com

I find it's very hard to think
Of pretty things to say,
So I'll just send a loving wish
For a merry Christmas day

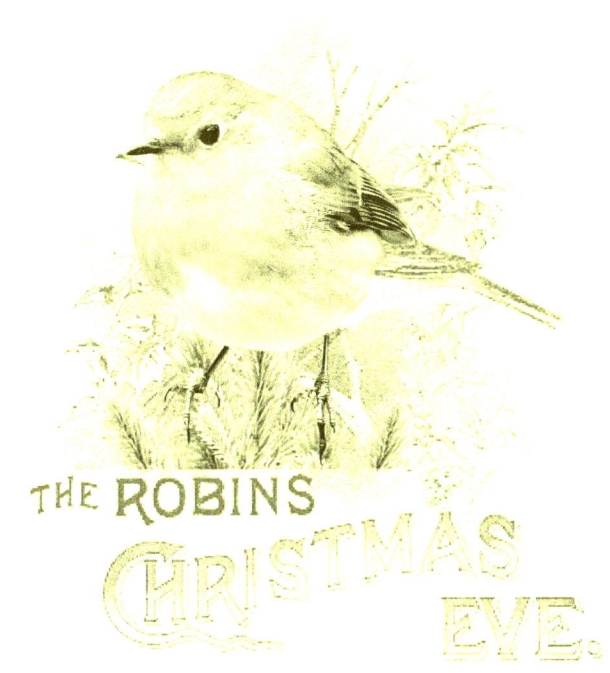

THE ROBINS
CHRISTMAS EVE.

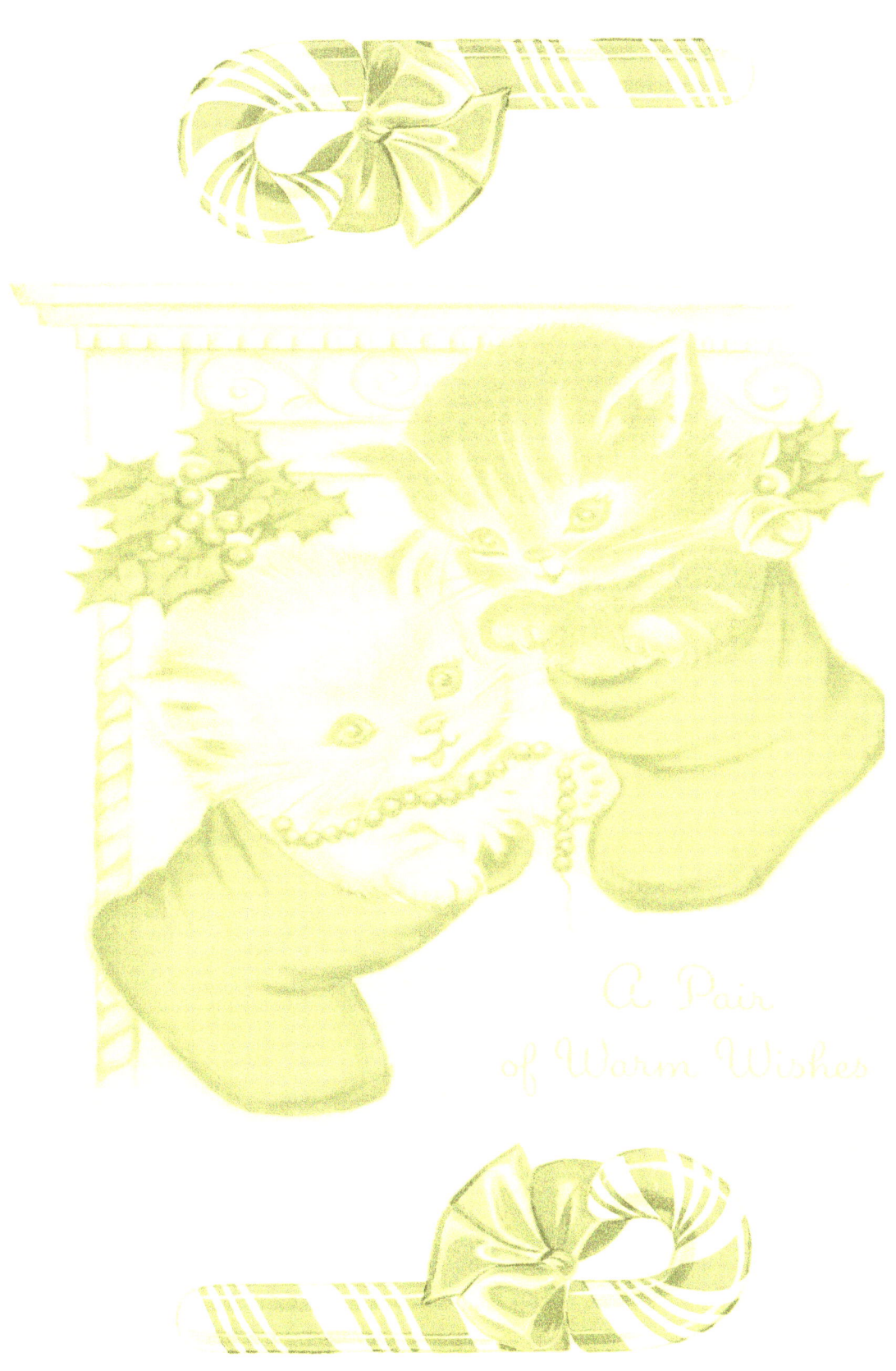

A Pair
of Warm Wishes

www.CreativeEmpires.com

www.CreativeEmpires.com

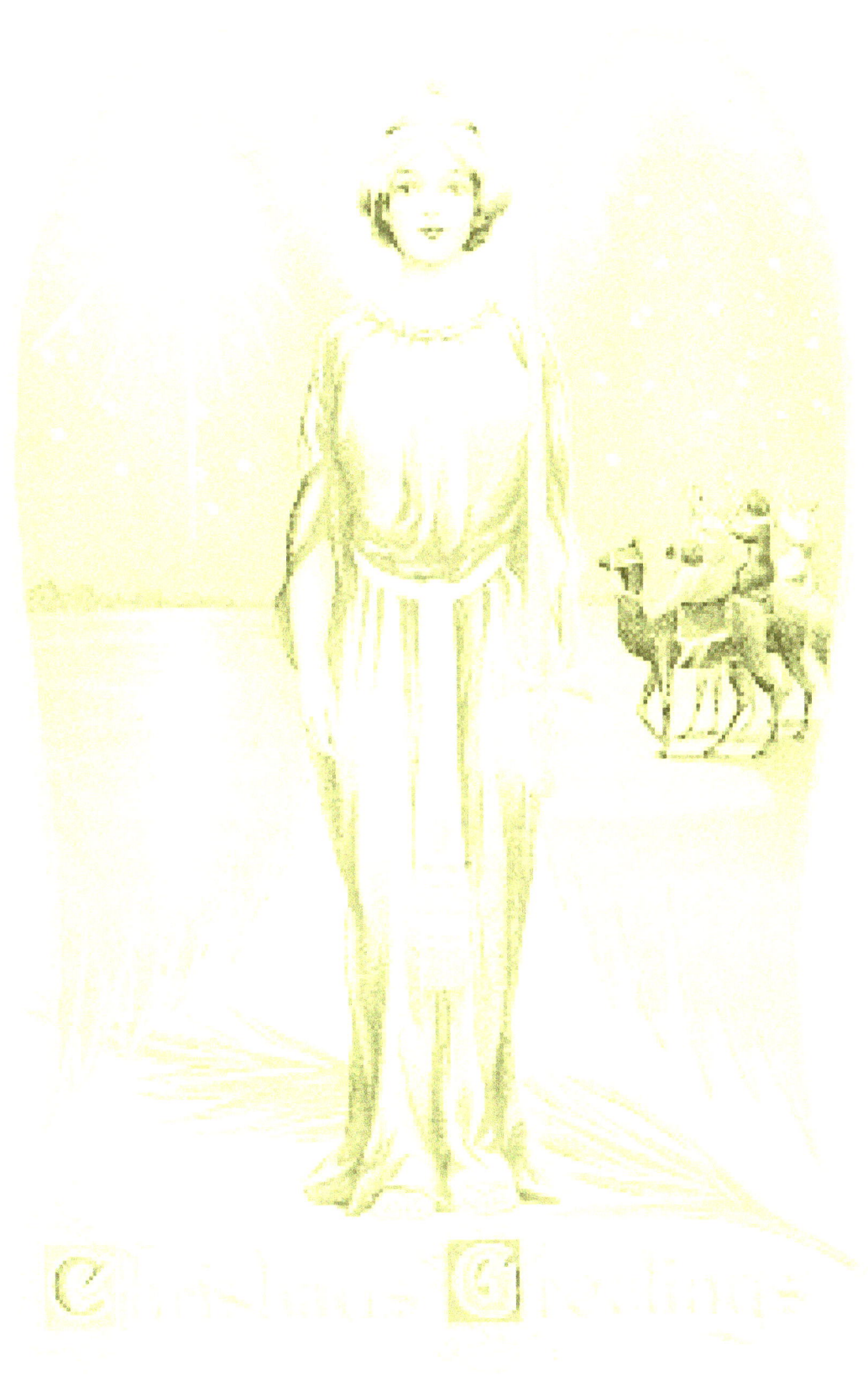

Christmas Greetings

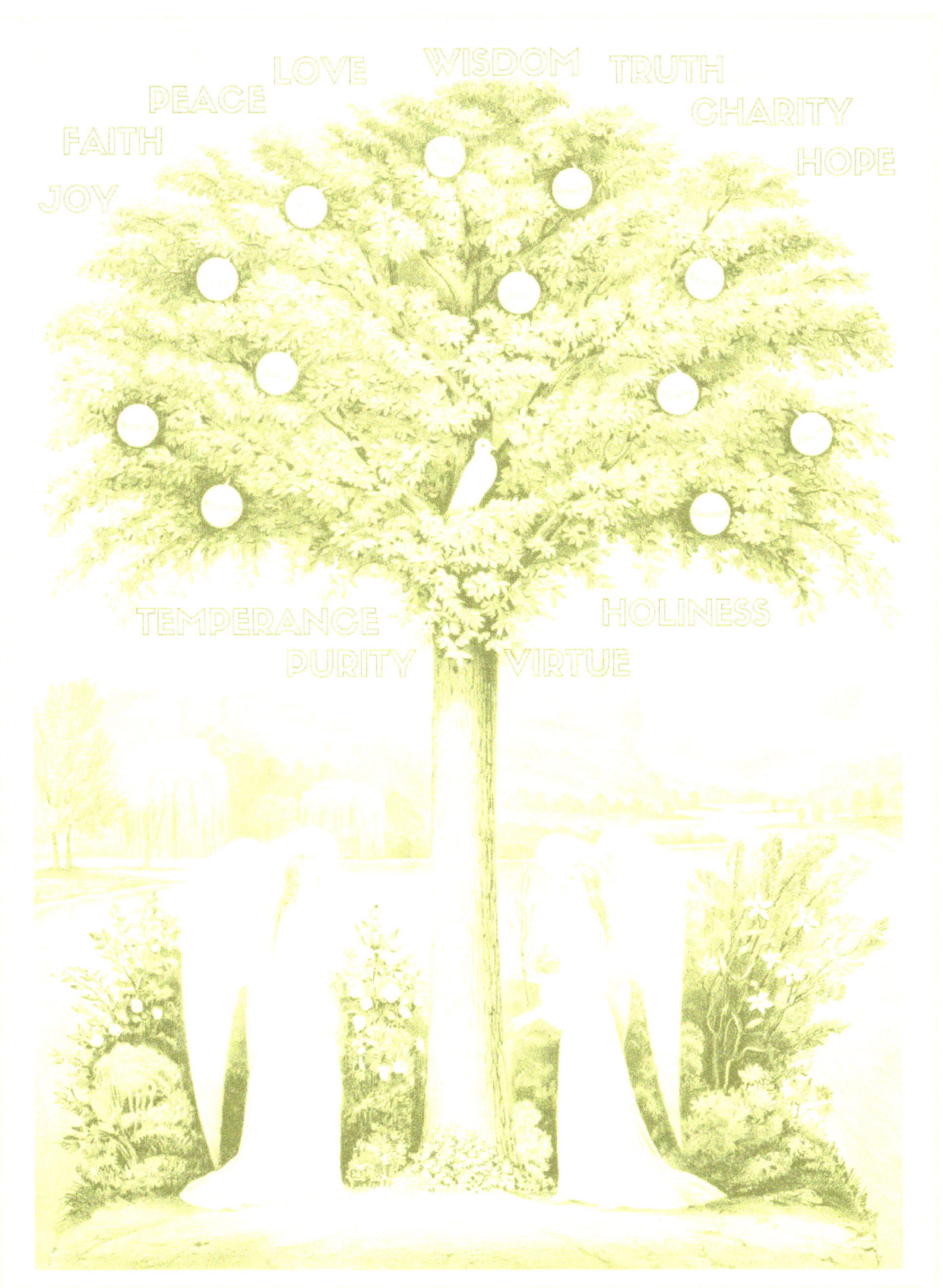

FAITH PEACE LOVE WISDOM TRUTH CHARITY HOPE JOY

TEMPERANCE HOLINESS PURITY VIRTUE

www.CreativeEmpires.com

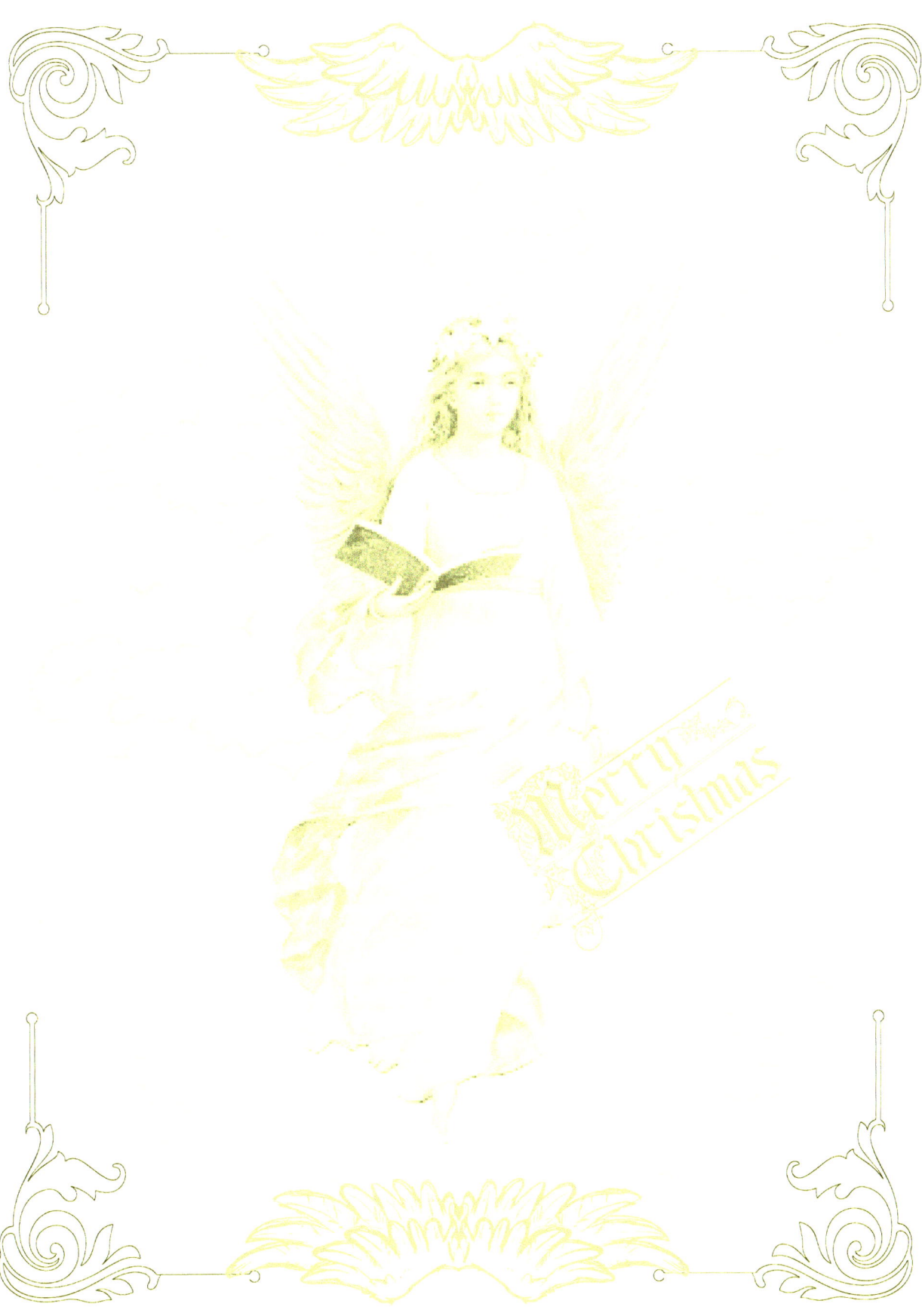

Merry Christmas

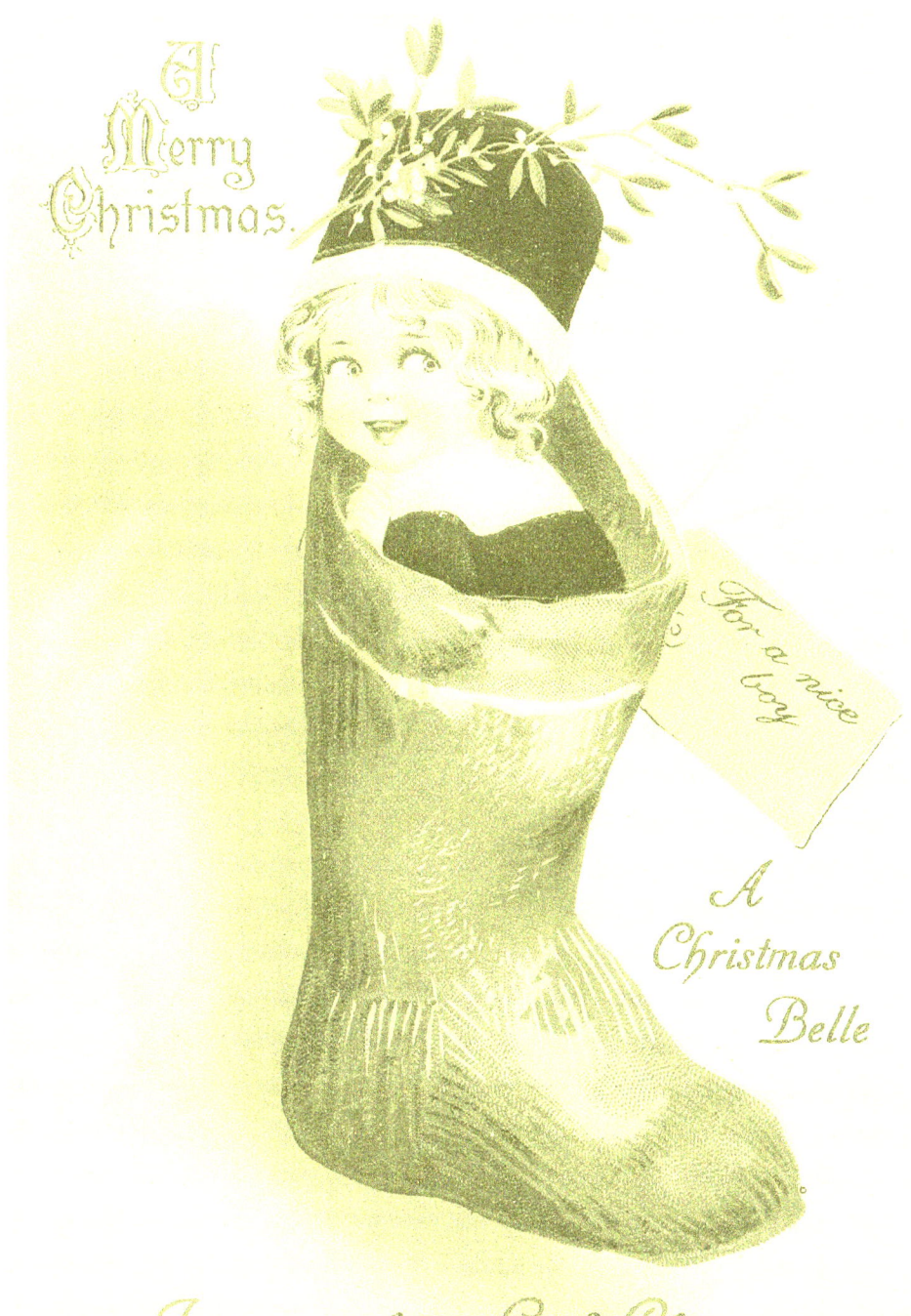

A
Merry
Christmas.

For a nice boy

A
Christmas
Belle

Just to wish you Good Cheer,
This glad time of the year.

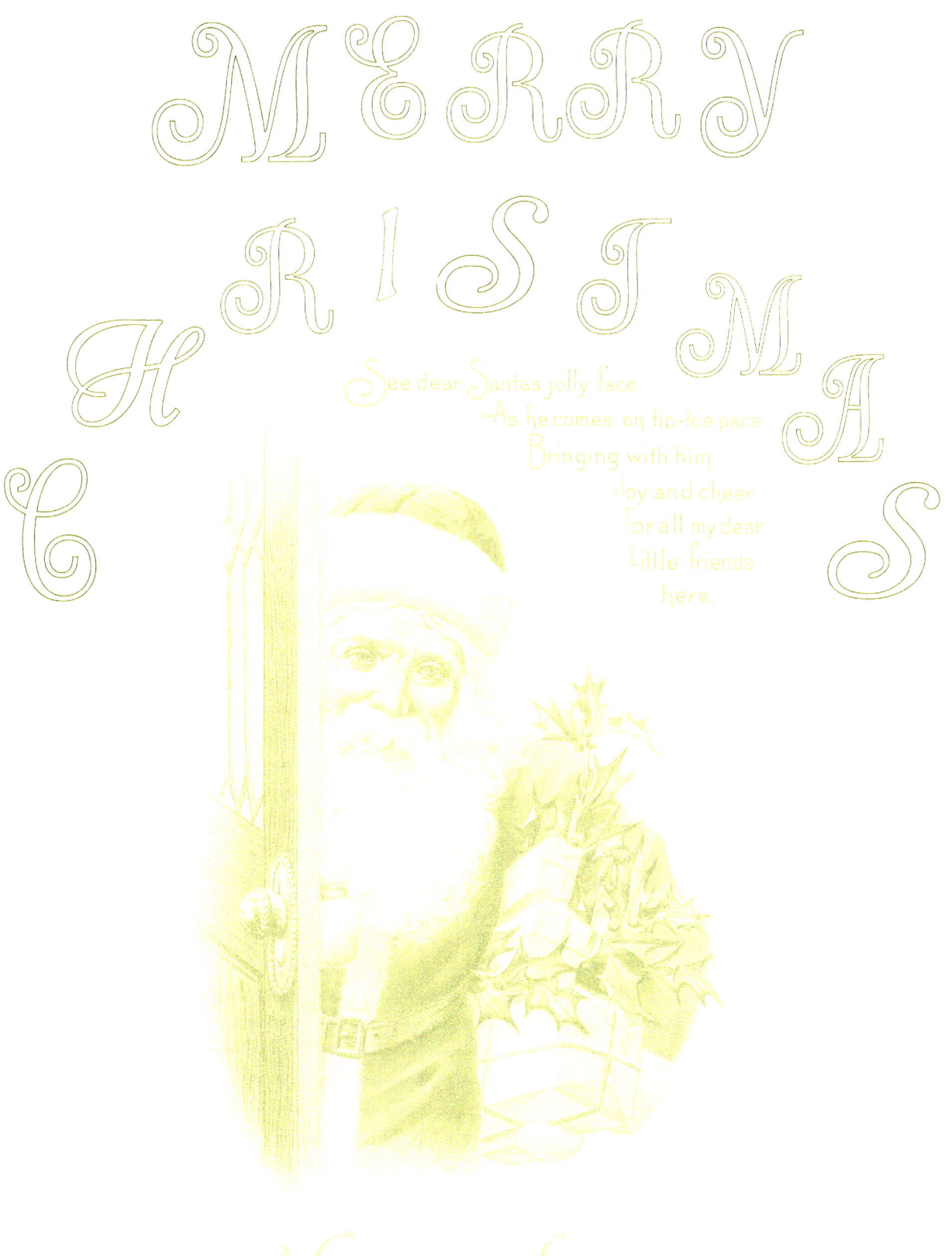

MERRY CHRISTMAS

See dear Santa's jolly face
As he comes on tip-toe pace
Bringing with him
Joy and cheer
For all my dear
Little friends
here.

A CHRISTMAS GREETING

www.CreativeEmpires.com

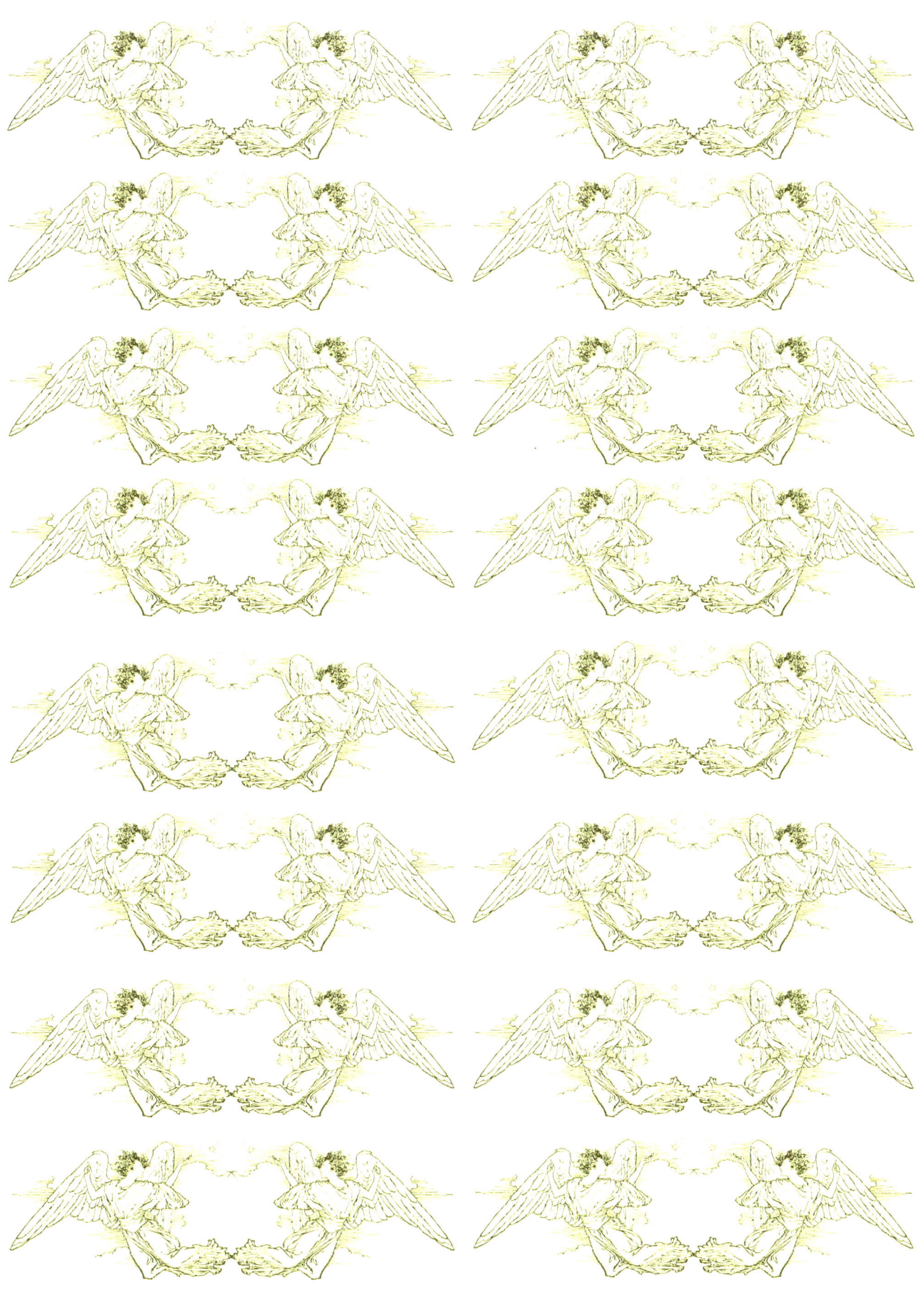

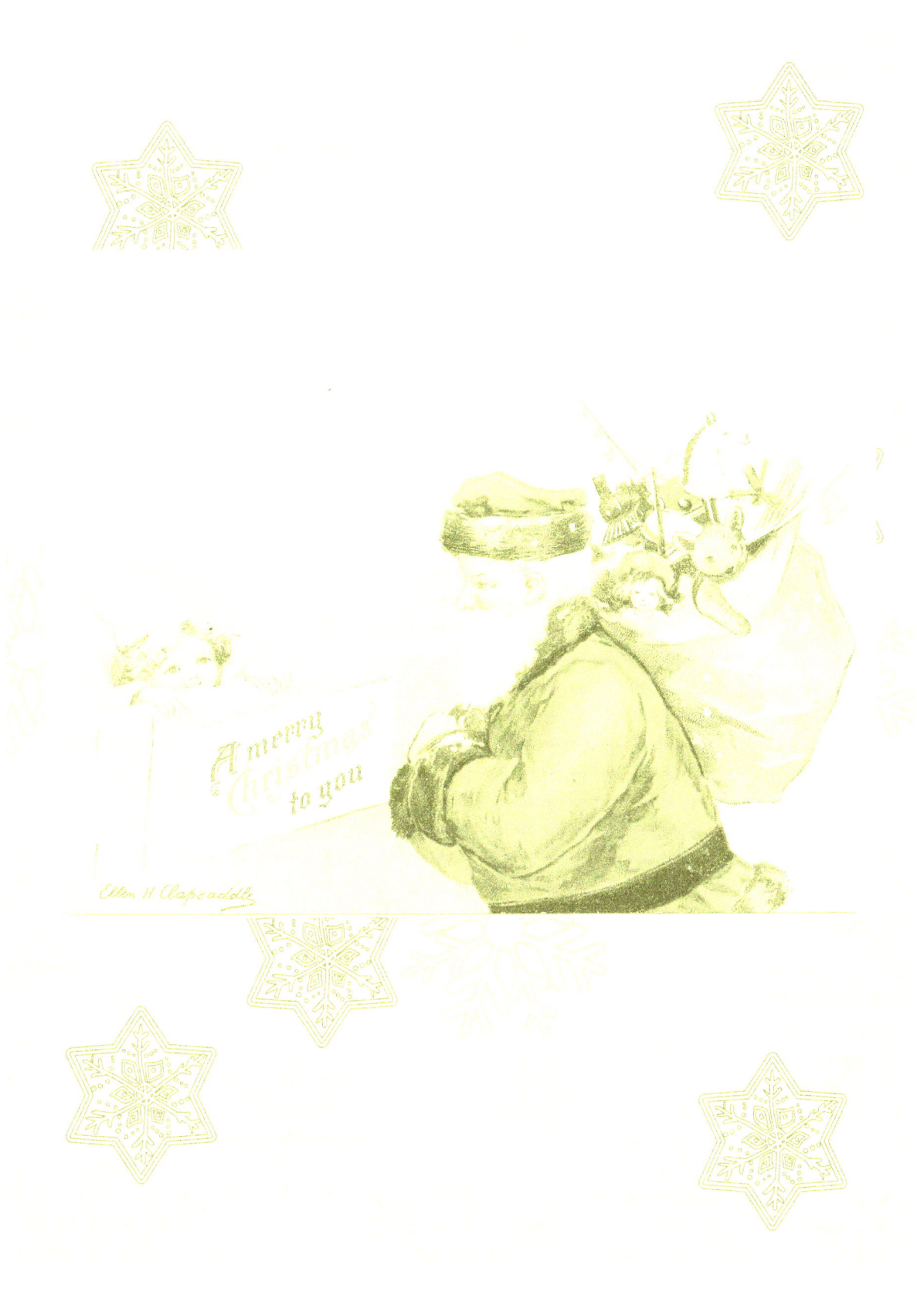

www.CreativeEmpires.com

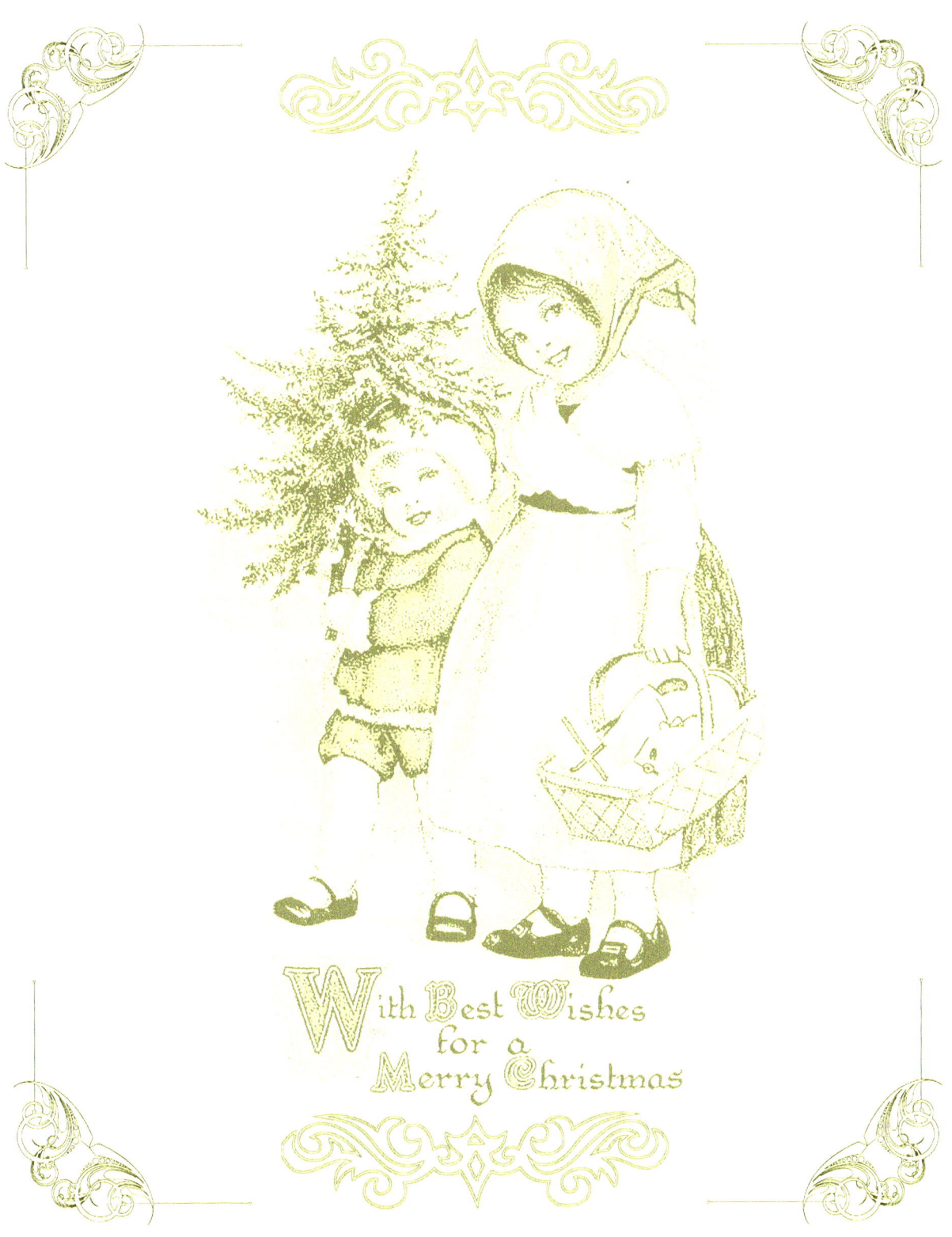

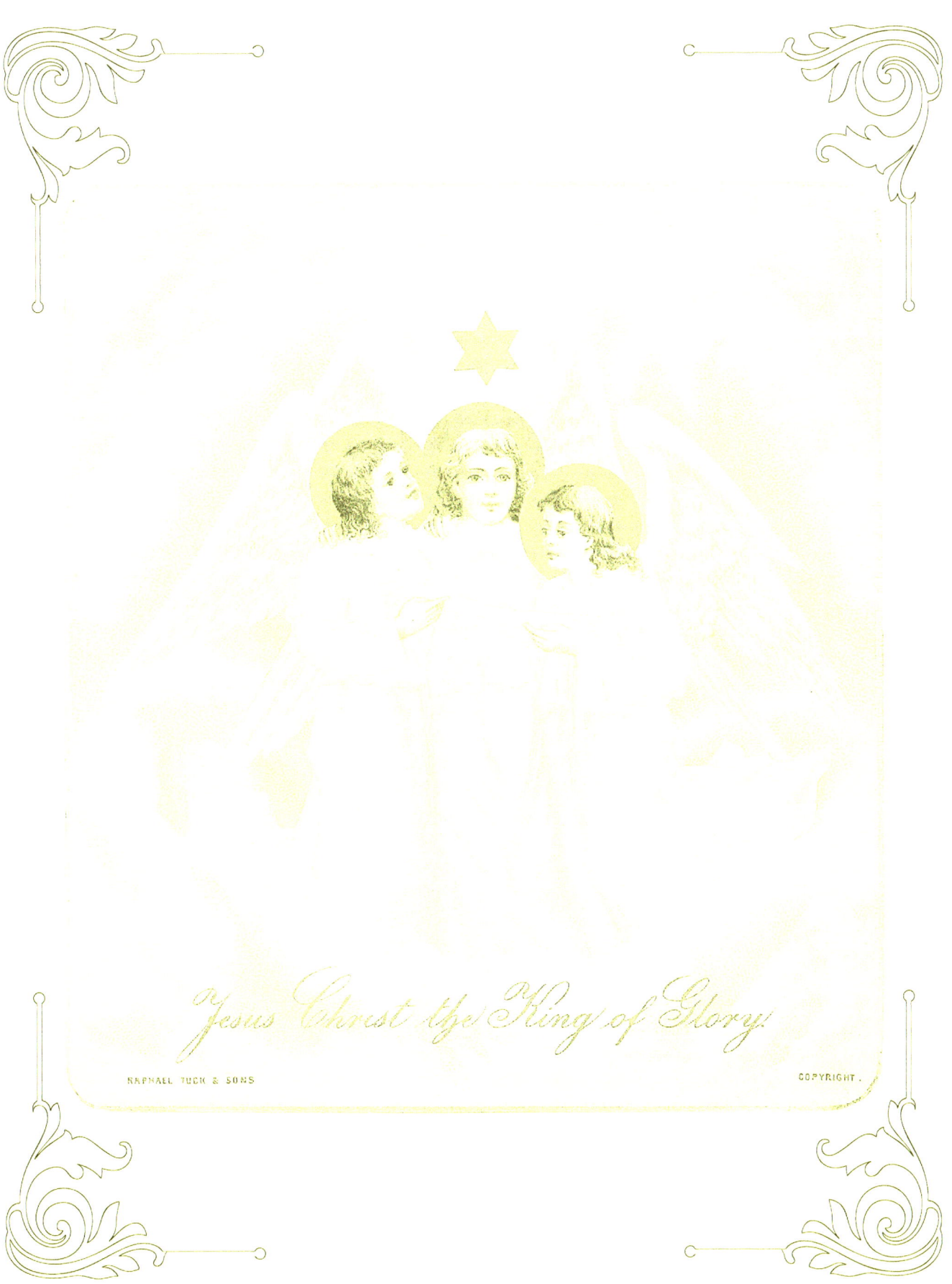

Jesus Christ the King of Glory.

RAPHAEL TUCK & SONS

COPYRIGHT.

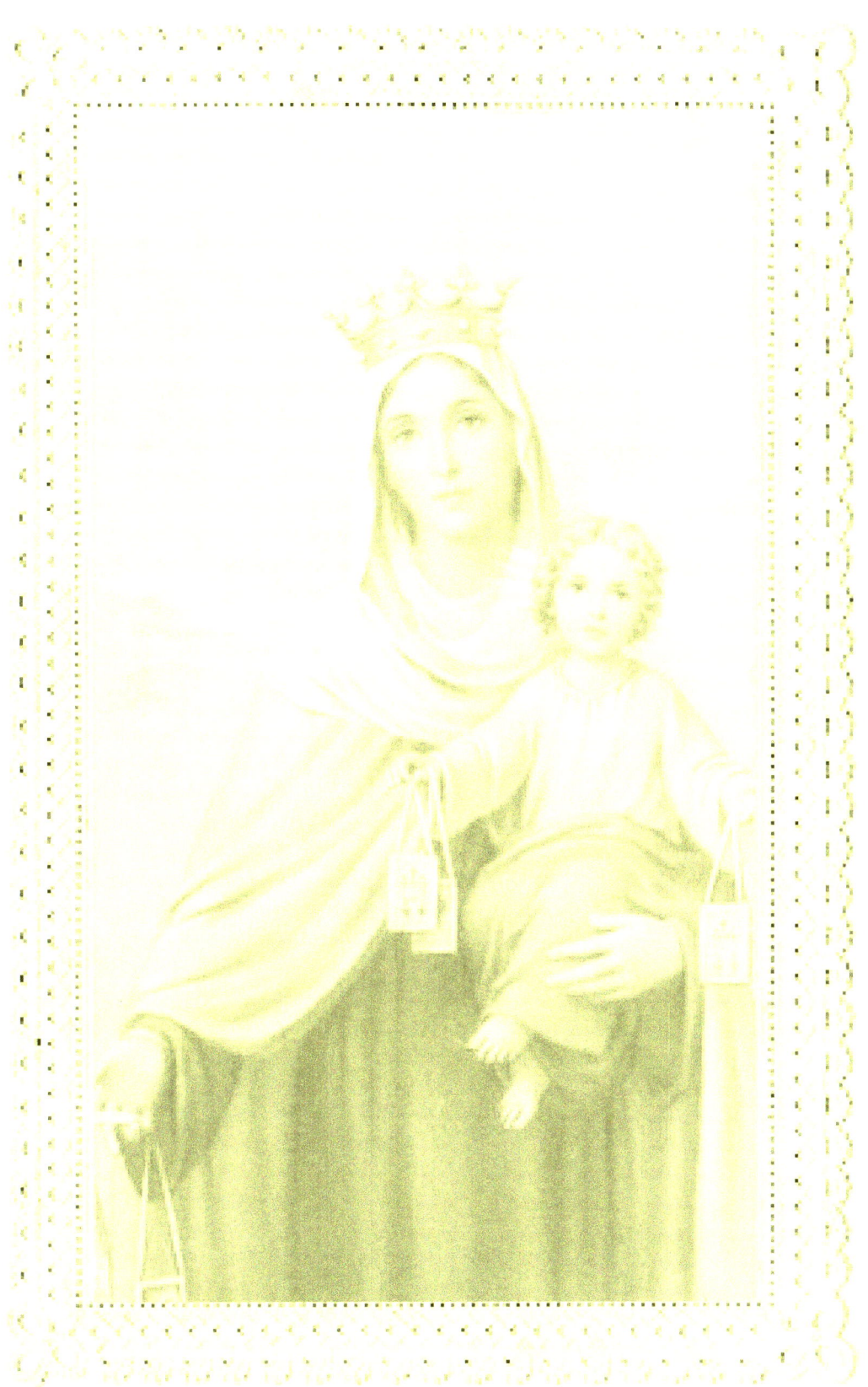

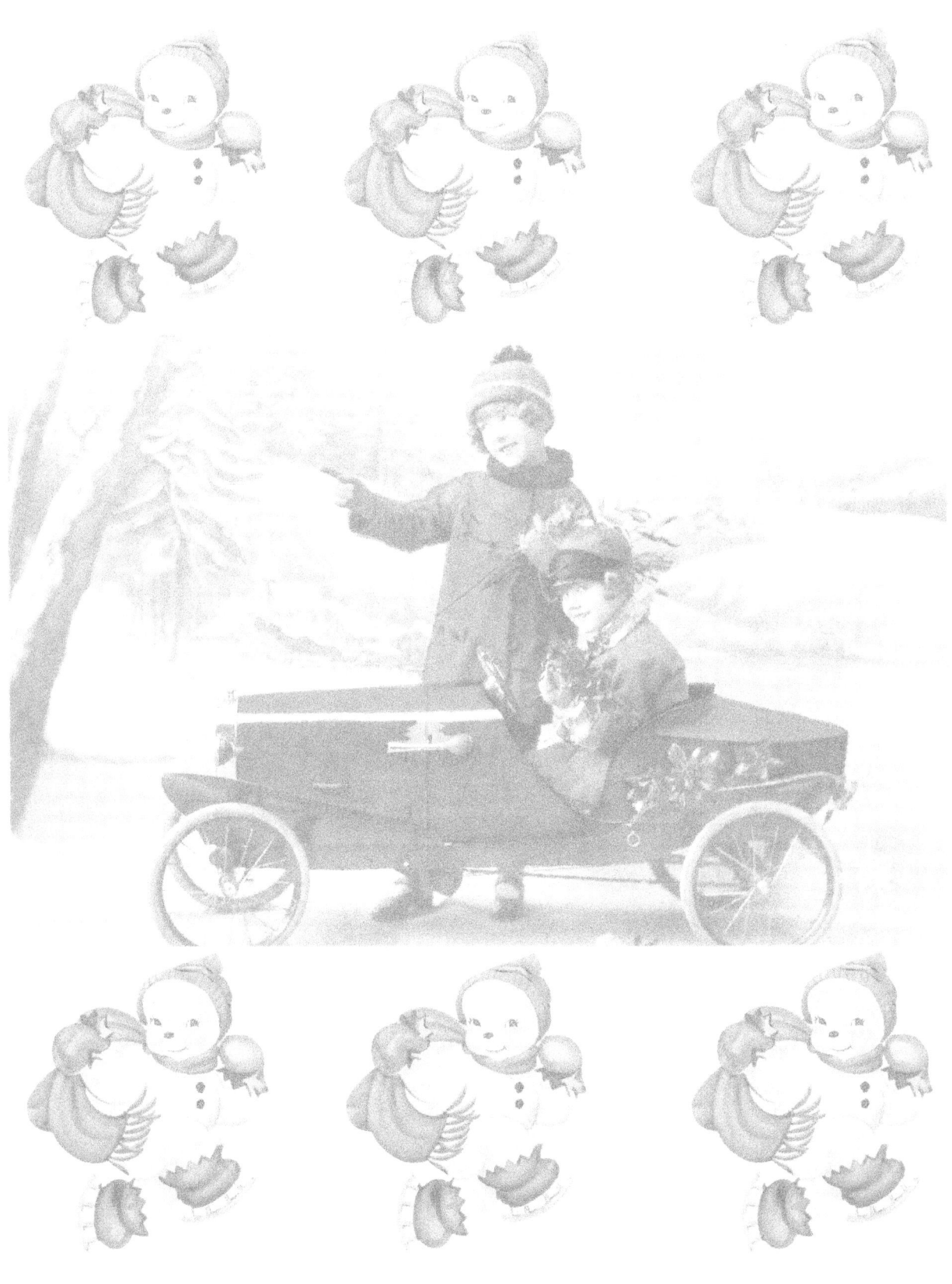

Letter To Santa

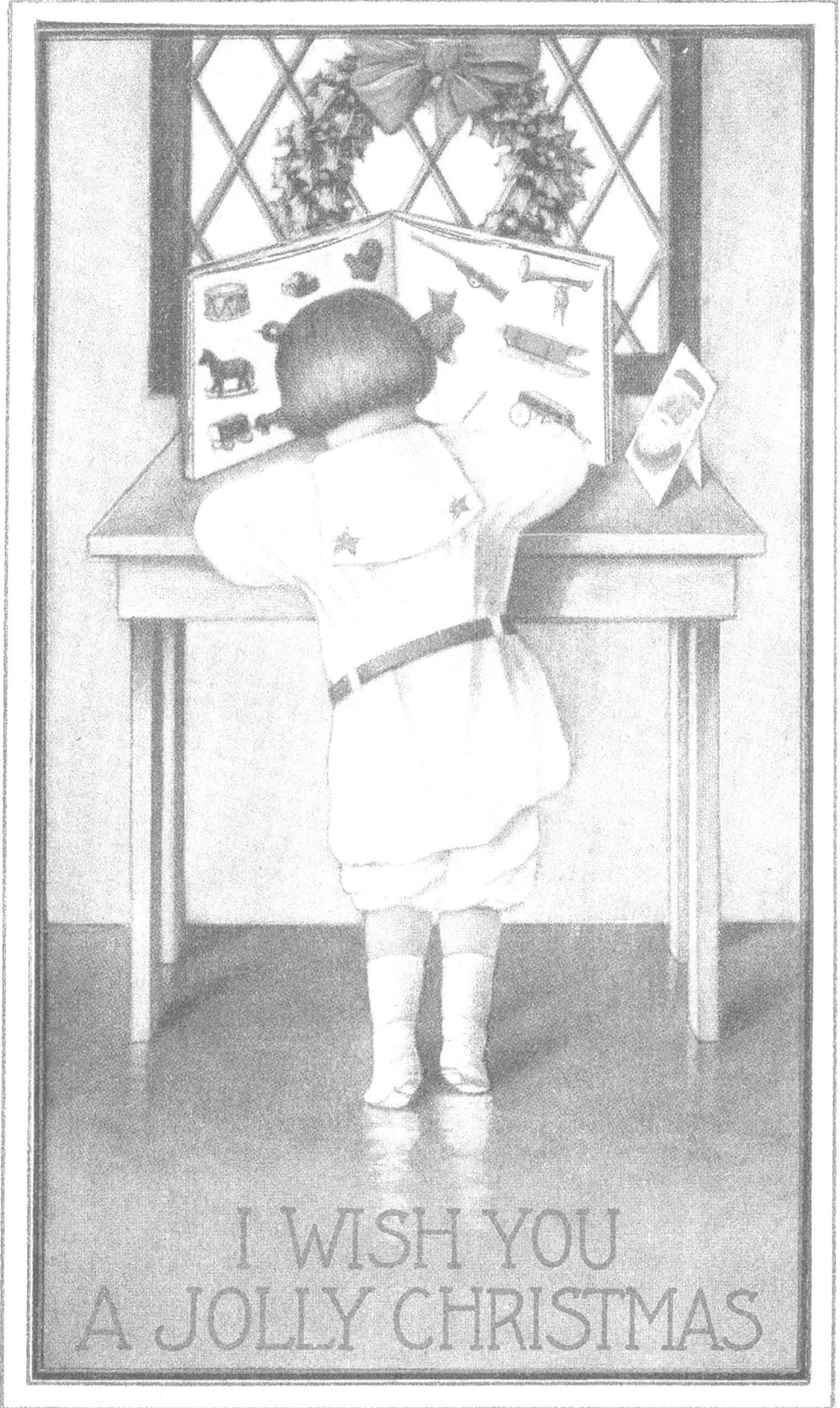

I WISH YOU
A JOLLY CHRISTMAS

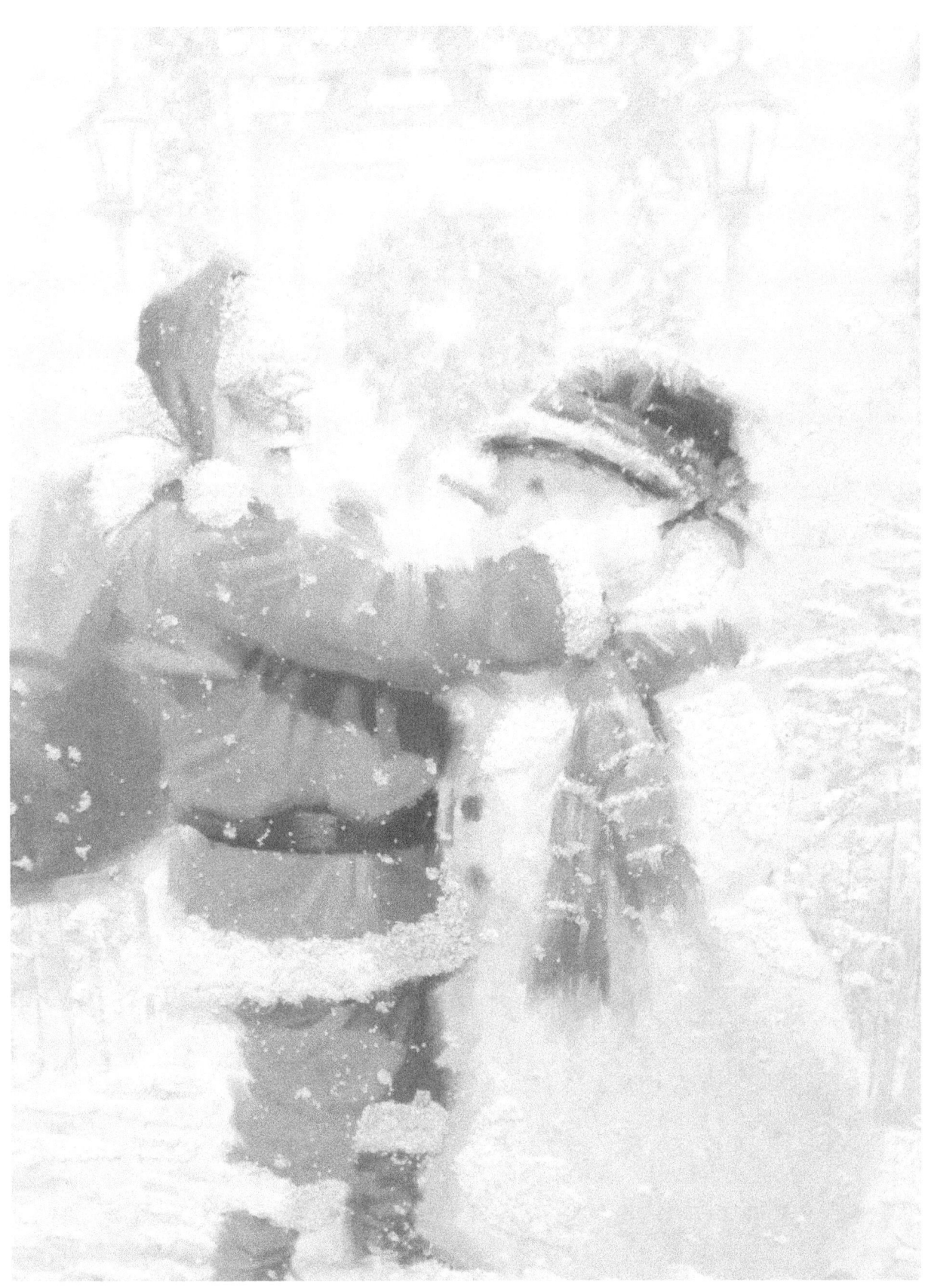

THANK

YOU

We really appreciate your

Support & Custom

Tracey, Shea & Rory

BY

CREATIVE

EMPIRES

PLEASE VISIT OUR WEBSITE
FOR DETAILS ON OUR OTHER PUBLICATIONS

WWW.CREATIVEMPIRES.COM

www.ingramcontent.com/pod-product-compliance
Lightning Source LLC
Chambersburg PA
CBHW062359220526
45472CB00008B/1872